FELLOWSHIP FOR TODAY
LENDING LIBRARY

You are preparing a permanent record for our library, so please print or write legibly.

Christian Healing
Title

Fillmore, Charles
Author (Last, First)

☑ Book ☐ CD/Tape ☐ DVD/Video

☐ Other (Please specify): _____

This item is a: ☑ Gift ☐ Loan

UN
Category

Given by _____

Date given

CHRISTIAN HEALING

Charles Fillmore

UNITY SCHOOL OF CHRISTIANITY
UNITY VILLAGE, MO 64065

ISBN 0-87159-017-4

PREFACE

These are not simply lectures; they are, rather, lessons. They are not merely to be read; they are to be studied and applied as one studies and applies mathematical rules.

When the text suggests that the reader "hold a thought," or affirm or deny a certain proposition, the student should stop reading, and both audibly and mentally do as bidden. This will set up new thought currents in mind and body, and will make way for the spiritual illumination that will follow in all who are faithful to these instructions.

The statements following each lesson should be used for mental discipline. Write these statements down and apply them daily while studying the lesson to which they correspond. Anyone can do spiritual healing who will use the simple rules of denial and affirmation here set forth. If you wish to heal another, hold him in mind and mentally repeat the denials and affirmations; this will raise your consciousness to spiritual reality, where all healing power originates. If you wish to heal yourself, talk to your mind and body as you would talk to a patient.

CONTENTS

The True Character of Being

LESSON ONE

1. "There is a spirit in man, and the breath of the Almighty giveth them understanding." The science that is here set forth is founded upon Spirit. It does not always conform to intellectual standards, but it is, nevertheless, scientific. The facts of Spirit are of a spiritual character and, when understood in their right relation, they are orderly. Orderliness is law, and is the test of true science.

2. The lawful truths of Spirit are more scientific than the constantly shifting opinions based on intellectual standards. The only real science is the science of Spirit. It never changes. It is universally accepted by all who are in Spirit, but one must be "in the Spirit" before one can understand this science of Spirit. The mind of Spirit must become active in those who would grasp the orderly science of Being that these lessons proclaim.

3. It is not absolutely necessary that the spiritual part of man's nature be active at the beginning of his study of this science. The primal object of the lessons is to quicken the spiritual realm of consciousness and to bring about the "breath of the Almighty" that gives understanding.

4. So let it be understood that we are teaching the science of Spirit, and that those who are receptive to the teaching will be inspired to spiritual consciousness. It is not difficult to accomplish, this

receiving the "breath" or inspiration of Spirit. We all
are inspired by Spirit, in certain states of consciousness. Understanding of the laws governing the realm
of Spirit will make it possible to attain this consciousness and to receive this inspiration whenever
requirements are met.

5. The starting point in spiritual realization is
a right understanding of that One designated as
the Almighty. It is strictly logical and scientific to
assume that man comes forth from this One, who
is named variously, but who, all agree, is the origin
of everything. Since man is the offspring of the
Almighty, he must have the character of his Parent.
If the earthly child resembles his parents, how much
more should the heavenly child resemble his Parent.
The truth that God is the Father of man does away
with the oft proclaimed presumption that it is impossible for the finite to understand the Infinite.
God must be in His universe as everywhere intelligent power; otherwise, it would fall to pieces. God
is in the universe as its constant "breath" or inspiration; hence it is only necessary to find the point of
contact in order to understand the One in whom we
all "live, and move, and have our being."

6. A sense of logic is a fundamental constituent
of man's being, and all minds acquiesce in statements
of logical sequence. We all see the relation and
unity of cause and effect, mentally stated, but, because the realm of forms does not always carry out
our premise, we fall away from the true standard

and try to convince ourselves that our logic is, somehow, defective. The one important thing that the student of spiritual science must learn is to trust the logic of mind. If appearances are out of harmony with your mental premise, do not let them unseat your logic. "Judge not according to appearance, but judge righteous judgment." You would not take the mixed figures of a child working a problem in mathematics as an example of the trueness of the principle; nor could you detect an error in the problem unless you were somewhat familiar with the rules of mathematics. Mental propositions are the standards and governing principles in all sciences developed by man. In the science of creation the same rule holds good. You may rest in the assurance that the principles that you mentally perceive as true of God are inviolate, and that, if there seems to be error in their outworking, it is because of some misapplication on the part of the demonstrator. By holding to the principle and insisting upon its accuracy, you open the way to a fuller understanding of it; you will also be shown the cause of the errors in the demonstration.

7. Then, if you have been in confusion mentally through contemplation of a world both good and evil, and have, in consequence, got into skeptical ways, the only true remedy is to stand by the pure reason of your spiritual perception and let it clear up the proposition for you. Dismiss all prejudices based upon the mixed perception; make your mind

receptive to the clearer understanding that will surely
appear when you have taken sides with Spirit, when
you look to Spirit alone for the outworking of the
problem.

8. This is not blind belief; it is, in the superconsciousness, an acquiescence in the logic of Being.
The superconsciousness is man's only sure guide in
the mazes of the creative process. By trusting to the
infallibility of this guide, man opens himself to the
inspiration of the Almighty. Spirituality may be cultivated by, and the deep things of God may be revealed to, anyone who will mentally proclaim and
affirm the logical perception of the goodness and
the Truth of Being.

9. The central proposition in the inspiration of
Spirit is that God, or primal Cause, is good. It does
not make any great difference what you name this
primal Cause; the important consideration is a right
concept of its character. The Hindu calls it Brahma,
a being of such stupendous proportions that man
shrinks into nothingness in contemplating it. Although this greatness of absolute Being is true,
there is also another point of view—the smallness
of that same Being as evidenced in the presence of
its life in the most insignificant creations. So, in
order to get at the very heart of Being, it is necessary
to realize that it is manifesting in the least as well as
in the greatest, and that, in the bringing forth of a
universe, not one idea could be taken away without
unbalancing the whole. This brings us to a fuller

realization of our importance in the universe and to the necessity of finding our right place. It also puts us into very close touch with the Father of all, the one omnipresent Intelligence pervading everything.

10. The Father within you, so lovingly and familiarly revealed by Jesus, is not at a distance, far away in a place called "heaven." His abode is in the spiritual realms that underlie all creative forces. As Jesus realized and taught, "the kingdom of God is within you." Spirit is the seat of power; its abode is on the invisible side of man's nature.

11. This revelation of God immanent in the universe was clearly set forth by Paul: "over all, and through all, and in all." The inspired ministers of all times have proclaimed the same.

12. The Power that creates and sustains the universe includes in its activity the creating and the sustaining of man. The desire for a fuller understanding of this Power has awakened a great inquiry into the character of the all-pervading One. On every hand men are earnestly seeking to know about God, seeking to come into harmonious relation with Him. Some are succeeding, while others seem to make but little progress. The diversity of results obtained is caused by the variety of ways of approaching the one Mind—for such God is. In mind is the key to the whole situation, and when man clearly discerns the science of mind, he will solve easily all the mysteries of creation.

13. The dictionary definitions of *mind* and *spirit*

are nearly identical; with this analogy realized, we much more easily get in touch with God. If *spirit* and *mind* are synonymous, we readily perceive that there is no great mystery about spiritual things, that they are not far removed from our daily thoughts and experiences. "Ye are a temple of God, and . . . the Spirit of God dwelleth in you," simply means that God dwells in us as our mind dwells in our body. Thus we see that God creates and moves creation through the power of mind. The vehicles of mind are thoughts, and it is through our mind in thought action that we shall find God and do His will.

14. There are mental laws that investigators are discovering, observing, and tabulating as never before in the world's history. Man has the ability to discern and understand the various factors entering into the creative processes of mind, and he is, through the study of mental laws, perceiving and accepting the science of ideas, thoughts, and words. But those who investigate nature and her laws from the intellectual and physical viewpoint fall short of complete understanding, because they fail to trace back to the causing Mind the multitudinous symbols that make up the visible universe. The material forms that we see about us are the chalk marks of a mighty problem being outworked by the one Mind. To comprehend that problem and to catch a slight glimpse of its meaning, we must grasp the ideas that the chalk marks represent; this is what we mean by

studying Mind back of nature. Man is mind and he is capable of comprehending the plan and the detailed ideas of the supreme Mind.

15. Divine ideas are man's inheritance; they are pregnant with all possibility, because ideas are the foundation and cause of all that man desires. With this understanding as a foundation, we easily perceive how "all . . . mine are thine." All the ideas contained in the one Father-Mind are at the mental command of its offspring. Get behind a thing into the mental realm where it exists as an inexhaustible idea, and you can draw upon it perpetually and never deplete the source.

16. With this understanding of the potentiality of primal Cause, we find it a simple matter to work the problem of life—the key to the situation being *ideas.* Thus life in expression is activity; in Being it is an idea of activity. To make life appear on the visible plane, we have but to open our mind and our thoughts to the divine idea of life and activity, and lo, all visibility is obedient to us. It is through this understanding, and its cultivation in various degrees, that men have acquired the ability to raise dead bodies. Jesus understood this realm of supreme ideas, or, as He termed it, "the kingdom of God . . . within you." When He raised Lazarus He invoked this power. When Martha talked about a future resurrection, He said, "I am the resurrection, and the life: he that believeth on me, though he die, yet shall he live." One who identifies his whole mind

with omnipresent Mind becomes so much at one with it that he can overcome death.

17. The real of the universe is held in the mind of Being as ideas of life, love, substance, intelligence, Truth, and so forth. These ideas may be combined in a multitude of ways, producing infinite variety in the realm of forms. There is a right combination, which constitutes the divine order, the kingdom of heaven on earth. This right relation of ideas and the science of right thought is practical Christianity.

18. The student in the science of Being should start all his investigations and mental activities from the one-Mind foundation. If you are skeptical about the existence of God, or if you are an abstract believer in God without having had any experience or conscious mental awakening that has given you proof, you should be very industrious in prayer, affirmation, and invocation. Remember, God is not a king who can force his presence upon you whether you will or not, but an omnipresent Mind enfolding and interpenetrating all things.

19. There are goodness everlasting and joy beyond expression in a perfect union between your mind and this perfect Mind. The point of contact is a willingness and a seeking on your part. "Seek, and ye shall find; knock, and it shall be opened unto you."

20. This question naturally presents itself: If we are offspring of Divine Mind, why are we not nat-

urally conscious of its presence? The answer to this is: In using the privilege of our inheritance—the power to make ideas visible as things—we have created a realm that separates us in consciousness from the Father-Mind. This is the teaching of Jesus in the parable of the prodigal son. When we are weary of the sense consciousness, we have only to turn our face (intelligence) toward our Father's house; there we shall meet a loving welcome.

21. The understanding that God is not in a distant heaven, nor located in any way geographically, gives us a feeling of nearness to and unity with the parent Mind. This intercommunion of the man consciousness with the omnipresent spiritual force of the universe was beautifully exemplified by Jesus. God was closer to Him than hands or feet. He referred all things to this loving Father, who was in constant communion and cooperation with the Son; yet there was, even in His case, the independent personal consciousness that beset Him when He sought to be free from mortal limitations. So we should not be discouraged or cast down if we do not quickly find the kingdom of God within us. Jesus spent whole nights in prayer; we should not be weary with a few moments each day. A daily half hour of meditation will open up the mind to a consciousness of the inner One and will reveal many things that are hidden from the natural man.

22. The fact is, Truth cannot be imparted—it must be individually experienced. The presence of

Divine Mind in the soul cannot be told in words;
it can be hinted at and referred to in parable and
likened to this or to that, but it can never be described as it is. The ability of the individual mind
to combine the ideas of Divine Mind in a consciousness of its own makes each of us the "only begotten
Son," a particular and special creation. No two individuals in all the universe are exactly alike, because
there is always diversity in the ideas appropriated
by each individual from Divine Mind.

23. The truth is, then:

That God is Principle, Law, Being, Mind, Spirit,
All-Good, omnipotent, omniscient, omnipresent, unchangeable, Creator, Father, Cause, and source of
all that is;

That God is individually formed in consciousness
in each of us, and is known to us as "Father" when
we recognize Him within us as our Creator, as our
mind, as our life, as our very being;

That mind has ideas and that ideas have expression; that all manifestation in our world is the
result of the ideas that we are holding in mind and
are expressing;

That to bring forth or to manifest the harmony
of Divine Mind, or the "kingdom of heaven," all
our ideas must be one with divine ideas, and must
be expressed in the divine order of Divine Mind.

STATEMENTS FOR THE REALIZATION OF
DIVINE MIND

(To be used in connection with Lesson One)

1. *There is one Presence, one Intelligence, one Substance, one Life: the good omnipotent.*

2. *God is the name of the everywhere-present Principle, in whom I live, move, and have my being.*

3. *God is the name of my good.*

4. *God almighty, "Father of all, who is over all, and through all, and in all."*

5. *Thy name is Spirit. I know Thee as the one, the all-seeing, Mind.*

6. *"Our Father who art in heaven [the everywhere-present inner harmony], Hallowed be thy name [wholeness manifests Thy character]."*

7. *Thou art always with me as indwelling wisdom and love.*

8. *Thy law is now the standard of my life, and I am at peace.*

9. *"I in thee . . . and thou in me."*

10. *Thou art never absent from me—I now see Thee face to face.*

11. *I think Thy thoughts after Thee.*

12. *I dwell in Thee and share Thine omnipotence.*

13. *In Thee is my perfection.*

Being's Perfect Idea

1. The foundation of our religion is Spirit, and there must be a science of Truth. The science of Truth is God thinking out creation. God is the original Mind in which all real ideas exist. The one original Mind creates by thought. This is stated in the first chapter of John:

2. In the beginning was the Word [Logos—thought-word], and the Word was with God, and the Word was God. The same was in the beginning with God. All things were made through him; and without him was not anything made that hath been made.

3. Eadie's Biblical Cyclopedia says: "The term *Logos* means thought expressed, either as an idea in mind or as vocal speech."

4. An understanding of the Logos reveals to us the law under which all things are brought forth— the law of mind action. Creation takes place through the operation of the Logos. God is *thinking* the universe into manifestation right now. Even He cannot create without law. The law of the divine creation is the order and harmony of perfect thought.

5. God-Mind expresses its thoughts so perfectly that there is no occasion for change, hence all prayers and supplications for the change of God's will to conform to human desires are futile. God does not change His mind, or trim His thought, to meet the conflicting opinions of mankind. Understanding the perfection of God thoughts, man must conform to

them; so conforming, he will discover that there is never necessity for any change of the will of God in regard to human affairs.

6. A key to God-Mind is with everyone—it is the action of the individual mind. Man is created the "image" and "likeness" of God; man is therefore a phase of God-Mind, and his mind must act like the original Mind. Study your own mind, and through it you will find God-Mind. In no other way can you get a complete understanding of yourself, of the universe, and of the law under which it is being brought forth. When you see the Creator thinking out His universe as the mathematician thinks out his problem, you will understand the necessity for the very apparent effort that nature makes to express itself; you will also understand why the impulse for higher things keeps welling up within your soul. God-Mind is living, acting thoughts. God-Mind is thinking in you; it is pushing your mind to grasp true ideas and carry them into expression.

7. It is therefore true, in logic and in inspiration, that man and the universe are within God-Mind as living, acting thoughts. God-Mind is giving itself to its creations, and those creations thus are evolving an independence that has the power to cooperate with, or to oppose, the original God will. It is then of vital importance to study the mind and understand its laws, because the starting point of every form in the universe is an idea.

8. Every man asks the question at some time,

"What am I?" God answers: "Spiritually you are
My idea of Myself as I see Myself in the ideal;
physically you are the law of My mind executing
that idea." "Great is the mystery of godliness," said
Paul. A little learning is a dangerous thing in the
study of Being. To separate oneself from the whole
and then attempt to find out the great mystery is like
dissecting inanimate flesh to find the source of life.

9. If you would know the mystery of Being, see
yourself in Being. Know yourself as an integral idea
in Divine Mind, and all other ideas will recognize
you as their fellow worker. Throw yourself out of
the Holy Trinity and you become an onlooker.
Throw yourself into the Trinity and you become its
avenue of expression. The Trinity is known com-
monly as Father, Son, and Holy Spirit; metaphys-
ically it is known as mind, idea, expression. These
three are one. Each sees itself as including the other
two, yet in creation separate. Jesus, the type man,
placed Himself in the Godhead, and said: "He that
hath seen me hath seen the Father." But, recogniz-
ing the supremacy of spiritual Principle, which He
was demonstrating, He said: "The Father is greater
than I."

10. Reducing the Trinity to simple numbers
takes away much of its mystery. When we say that
there is one Being with three attitudes of mind, we
have stated in plain terms all that is involved in the
intricate theological doctrine of the Trinity. The
priesthood has always found it profitable to make

complex that which is simple. When religion becomes an industry it has its trade secrets, and to the uninitiated they seem very great. Modern investigation of the character of the mind is taking away all the mysteries of Egyptian, Hindu, Hebrew, and many other religious and mystical systems of the past. Advocates of these systems are attempting to perpetuate their so-called secret knowledge through the occult societies springing up on every side in our day, but they meet with indifferent success. The modern Truth seeker takes very little on trust. Unless the claimant to occult lore can demonstrate his power in the world of affairs, people are suspicious of him. Religious awe for the priesthood, which is prevalent in Oriental countries, is lacking in the majority of Western people. In India, a yellow-robed holy man is regarded with reverence by both adults and children; in this country adults stare and small boys throw stones until he seeks the protection of the police. This seems irreverent, almost heathenish, yet it is the expression of an innate repudiation of everything that seeks to establish itself on any other foundation than that of practical demonstration.

11. The mind of God is Spirit, soul, body; that is, mind, idea, expression. The mind of man is Spirit, soul, body—not separate from God-Mind, but existing in it and making it manifest in an identity peculiar to the individual. Every man is building into his consciousness the three departments of God-Mind, and his success in the process is evidenced by the

harmony, in his consciousness, of Spirit, soul, and body. If he is all body, he is but one-third expressed. If to body he has added soul, he is two-thirds man, and if to these two he is adding Spirit, he is on the way to the perfect manhood that God designed. Man has neither Spirit, soul, nor body of his own—he has identity only. He can say, "I." He uses God Spirit, God soul, and God body, as his "I" elects. If he uses them with the idea that they belong to him, he develops selfishness, which limits his capacity and dwarfs his product.

12. In his right relation, man is the inlet and the outlet of an everywhere-present life, substance, and intelligence. When his "I" recognizes this fact and adjusts itself to the invisible expressions of the one Mind, man's mind becomes harmonious; his life, vigorous and perpetual; his body, healthy. It is imperative that the individual understand this relation in order to grow naturally. It must not only be understood as an abstract proposition, but it is necessary that he blend his life consciously with God life, his intelligence with God intelligence, and his body with the "Lord's body." Conscious identification must prevail in the whole man before he can be in right relation. This involves not only a recognition of the universal intelligence, life, and substance, but also their various combinations in man's consciousness. These combinations are, in the individual world, dependent for perfect expression upon man's recognition of and his loyalty to his origin—God-

Mind. Man is in God-Mind as a perfect idea. God-Mind is constantly trying to express in every man its perfect idea, the real and only man.

13. The perfect-man idea in God-Mind is known under various names in the many religious systems. The Krishna of the Hindu is the same as the Messiah of the Hebrews. All the great religions of the world are founded upon spiritual science, but not all of that science is understood by their followers. The Hebrews had been told again and again, by the spiritually wise, that a Messiah, or Christ man, would be born in their midst, but when He came they did not recognize Him, because of their lack of understanding. They understood only the letter of their religion. A similar lack of understanding prevails generally today. The Christ man, or perfect idea of God-Mind, is now being expressed and demonstrated by men and women as never before in the history of the race. Those who claim to be followers of the true religion should beware of putting the perfect-man idea out of their synagogues as the Jews put out Jesus Christ. The ancient Pharisees asked Jesus: "By what authority doest thou these things?" Modern Pharisees are repeating the same question. The substance of Jesus' answer was: "By their fruits ye shall know them." (Read Mt. 21:23-46.)

14. This perfect-idea-of-God man is your true self. God-Mind is, under the law of thought, constantly seeking to release its perfection in you. It is your spirit, and when you ask for its guidance and

place yourself, by prayer and affirmation, in mental touch with it, there is a great increase in its manifestation in your life. It has back of it all the powers of Being, and there is nothing that it cannot do if you give it full sway and make your thought strong enough to express the great forces that it is seeking to express in you.

15. A most important part of the law of mind action is the fact of thought-unity. It is absolutely necessary to understand the nature of this fact before one can demonstrate the power of the superconscious mind. Among our associates, we like and are attracted to those who understand and sympathize with our thoughts. The same law holds good in Divine Mind—its thoughts are drawn to and find expression in the minds of those who raise themselves to its thought standard. This means that we must think of ourselves as God thinks of us, in order to appreciate and to receive His thoughts and to bring forth the fruits. If you think of yourself as anything less than the perfect child of the perfect Parent, you lower the thought standard of your mind and cut off the influx of thought from Divine Mind. Jesus referred to this law when He said: "Ye therefore shall be perfect, as your heavenly Father is perfect."

16. When we go forth in the understanding of man's perfect nature, we find a new state of consciousness forming in us; we think and do many things not according to the established custom, and

the old consciousness rises up and asks: "By what authority?" We have so long looked for man-made authority in religious matters that we feel that we are treading on dangerous ground if we dare to think beyond prescribed doctrines. Right here we should appeal to the supreme reason of Spirit and proclaim what we perceive as the highest truth, regardless of precedent or tradition, mental ignorance or physical limitation: I AM is the "image of God," the "only begotten Son" (the expressed, *or pressed out*, Mind) of the Most High. This is our true estate, and we shall never realize it until we enter into it in *mind*, because there it is, and nowhere else.

17. Only through the superconscious mind can we behold and commune with God. "No man hath seen God at any time; the only begotten Son, who is in the bosom of the Father, he hath declared *him*." It is taught that Jesus was exclusively the "only begotten Son," but He Himself said: "Is it not written in your law, 'I said, Ye are gods'?" He proclaimed the unity of all men in the Father. "I am the light of the world." "Ye are the light of the world." Paul says, "As many as are led by the Spirit of God, these are sons of God." We are "heirs of God, and joint-heirs with Christ."

18. In this matter of sonship is one important point that we should not overlook; that point is the difference between those who perceive their sonship as a possibility, and those who have demonstrated it in their lives. "Ye must be born anew," was the

proclamation of Jesus. The first birth is the human—
the self-consciousness of man as an intellectual and
physical being; the second birth, the being "born
anew," is the transformation and translation of the
human to a higher plane of consciousness as the son
of God.

19. The second birth is that in which we "put
on Christ." It is a process of mental adjustment and
body transmutation that takes place right here on
earth. "Have this mind in you, which was also in
Christ Jesus," is an epitome of a mental and physical
change that may require years to work out. But all
men must go through this change before they can
enter into eternal life and be as Jesus Christ is.

20. This being "born anew," or "born from
above," is not a miraculous change that takes place
in man; it is the establishment in his consciousness
of that which has always existed as the perfect-man
idea in Divine Mind. God created man in His
"image" and "likeness." God being Spirit, the man
that He creates is spiritual. It follows as a logical
sequence that man, on the positive, formative, creative side of his nature, is the direct emanation of
his Maker; that he is just like his Maker; that he is
endowed with creative power, and that his very being is involved in God-Mind which he is releasing
by his creative thought. It is to this spiritual man
that the Father says: "All things that are mine are
thine."

21. Understanding of the status of all men in

Divine Mind gives us a new light upon the life of
Jesus of Nazareth and makes plain many of His
seemingly mysterious statements. This spiritual consciousness, or Christ Mind, was quickened in Him,
and through it He realized His relation to First
Cause. When asked to show the Father, whom He
constantly talked to as if He were personally present,
He said, "He that hath seen me hath seen the Father."
His personality had been merged into the universal.
The mind of Being and the thought of Being were
joined, and there was no consciousness of separation
or apartness.

22. Everything about man presages the higher
man. Foremost of these prophesies is the almost
universal desire for the freedom that spiritual life
promises, freedom from material limitations. The
immortal perception spurs man on to invent mechanical devices that will carry him above limitations.
For example, he flies by means external. In his spiritual nature he is provided with the ability to overcome gravity; when this power is developed, it will
be common to see men and women passing to and
fro in the air, without wings or mechanical appli-
ances of any description.

23. The human organism has a world of latent
energies waiting to be brought into manifestation.
Distributed throughout the body are many nerve
centers whose offices are as yet but vaguely understood. In the New Testament, which is a work on
spiritual physiology, these centers are referred to as

"cities" and "rooms." The "upper room" is the very
top of the head. Jesus was in this "upper room" of
His mind when Nicodemus came to see Him "by
night"—meaning the ignorance of sense consciousness. It was in this "upper room" that the followers
of Jesus prayed until the Holy Spirit came upon
them. The superconsciousness, or Christ Mind, finds
its first entrance into the natural mind through this
higher brain center. By thought, speech, and deed
this Christ Mind is brought into manifestation. The
new birth is symbolically described in the history of
Jesus.

24. "Verily I say unto you, that many prophets
and righteous men desired to see the things which
ye see, and saw them not; and to hear the things
which ye hear, and heard them not."

STATEMENTS FOR THE REALIZATION OF THE
SON OF GOD

(To be used in connection with Lesson Two)

1. *I am the son of God, and the Spirit of the Most High dwells in me.*

2. *I am the only begotten son, dwelling in the bosom of the Father.*

3. *I am the lord of my mind, and the ruler of all its thought people.*

4. *I am the Christ of God.*

5. *Through Christ I have dominion over my every thought and word.*

6. *I am the beloved son in whom the Father is well pleased.*

7. *Of a truth I am the son of God.*

8. *All that the Father has is mine.*

9. *He that hath seen me hath seen the Father.*

10. *I and my Father are one.*

11. *My highest ideal is a perfect man.*

12. *My next highest ideal is that I am that perfect man.*

13. *I am the image and likeness of God, in whom is my perfection.*

14. *It is written in the law of the Lord, "Ye are gods, and . . . sons of the Most High."*

15. *These are written, that ye may believe that Jesus is the Christ, the Son of God; and that believing ye may have life in his name.*

Manifestation

LESSON THREE

1. As a rule, religious people are not scientific. They think that religion and science are separated by a gulf, and that the scientific mind is spiritually dangerous. Science, to them, is associated with Darwin, Huxley, and other students of natural law who have been skeptical about the accuracy of the Bible from the standpoint of natural science, and whom, because of this skepticism, they brand as infidels. Hence it has come to be almost heresy for a good Christian to think about his religion as having a "scientific" side.

2. By science we mean the systematic and orderly arrangement of knowledge. This definition does not confine science to the facts of the material world. There is a science in Christianity, and it is only through the understanding of this science as a fundamental of Christianity that the Christ teachings can be fully demonstrated in the life of man. To fail to understand the science upon which spiritual understanding rests is to fail in nearly every demonstration of its power. Paul says: "I will pray with the spirit, and I will pray with the understanding also."

3. There is a gulf between the high spiritual understanding and the material manifestation. It is only by bridging this gulf that science and religion can be reconciled. The bridge needed is the structure that thought builds. When Christians under-

stand the science of thinking, the power of thought to manifest itself, and how the manifestation of thought is accomplished, they will no longer fear material science; when material scientists have fathomed the real nature of the living force that they even now discern as ever active in all nature's structures, they will have more respect for religion.

4. Both the religionist and the physicist incorrectly hold that the Bible is a historical description of man's creation. Beginning with the very first chapter of Genesis, the Bible is an allegory. It is so regarded by the majority of Hebrew scholars, and they certainly ought to know the character of their own Scriptures. Paul was a Hebrew, and thoroughly versed in the occultism of spiritual writings; he said, referring to the story of Abraham and Sarah, "Which things contain an allegory." Hebrews almost universally claim that the story of the Garden of Eden, Adam, Eve, and the serpent is symbology.

5. In the face of these facts, it seems strange that orthodox Christianity should insist that the Bible is a literal history. It is this literal viewpoint that has stood in the way of true spiritual understanding. Read in the light of Spirit, the 1st chapter of Genesis is a description, in symbol, of the creative action of universal Mind in the realm of ideas. It does not pertain to the manifest universe any more than the history of the inventor's idea pertains to the machine that he builds to manifest the idea. First the problem is thought out, and afterward the structure is

produced. So God builds His universe. This is explained in the 2d chapter of Genesis, which says that God "rested . . . from all his work," and yet there were no plants of the field, "and there was not a man to till the ground." "And Jehovah God formed man of the dust of the ground, and breathed into his nostrils the breath of life; and man became a living soul."

6. Only through perception of the mental law by which ideas manifest from the formless to the formed can we understand and reconcile these two apparently contradictory chapters. In the light of true understanding everything is made plain, and we discern just how Divine Mind is creating man and the universe: first the ideal concept, then the manifestation.

7. The six days of creation, as described in the 1st chapter of Genesis, represent six great ideal projections from Divine Mind, each more comprehensive than its predecessor. The final climax is reached in the sixth degree, when that phase of Being called man appears, having dominion over everything, or every idea, that has gone before. This ideal man, who is made in the "image" and "likeness" of Elohim, is the epitome and focal center around which all creation revolves; hence the one important study of man is the mind of man. In mind is the key to all mysteries, both religious and material. When we know how mind manifests from the ideal to the so-called real, we are no longer in the

dark, but have that Truth which Jesus said would make us free.

8. There is but one man. On the spiritual side of his being, every man in the universe has access to that man, eternally existing in Divine Mind as a perfect-man idea. When man appreciates this mighty truth and applies it in his conscious thinking, all manifestation becomes harmonious and orderly to him, and he sees God everywhere.

9. A right understanding of the divine law of creation reveals man as a necessary factor in God's great work. Through man, God is forming or manifesting outwardly that which exists in the ideal. In order, then, that the creation shall go on and be fulfilled as God has designed, man must not only understand the law of mind action in his individual thought, but he must also understand his relation to the universal thought. Not only must he understand it, but in his every thought he must consciously co-operate with divine ideals. Jesus understood this law and repeatedly claimed that He was sent of God to carry out the divine will in the world. This commission is given to every man, and man will not have satisfaction in life until he recognizes this universal law; until he becomes an obedient, willing co-worker with Divine Mind.

10. Spiritual man is I AM; manifest man is *I will*. I AM is the Jehovah God of Scripture, and *I will* is the Adam. It is the I AM man that forms and breathes into the *I will* man the "breath of life."

When we are in the realm of the ideal, we are I AM; when we are expressing ideals in thought or in act, we are *I will.* When the *I will* gets so absorbed in its realm of expression that it loses sight of the ideal and centers all its attention in the manifest, it is Adam listening to the serpent and hiding from Jehovah God. This breaks the connection between Spirit and manifestation, and man loses that spiritual consciousness which is his under divine law. In this state of mind the real source of supply is cut off, and there is a drawing upon the reserve forces of the organism, the tree of life. It is in this experience that man is described as being driven out of the Garden of Eden, or the paradise of Being.

11. Every idea projects form. The physical body is the projection of man's idea; we carry the body in the mind. The body is the fruit of the tree of life, which grows in the midst of the garden of mind. If the body-idea is grounded and rooted in Divine Mind, the body will be filled with a perpetual life flow that will repair all its imperfect parts and heal all its diseases.

12. When man realizes that there is but one body-idea and that the conditions in his body express the character of his thought, he has the key to bodily perfection and immortality in the flesh. But "flesh and blood cannot inherit the kingdom of God." The "flesh and blood" here referred to is the corruptible-body idea that men carry in mind. When we get the right idea of the origin and character of the body,

the corruptible will put on incorruption and our bodies will be raised from the dead, as was the body of Jesus. "Neither was he left unto Hades, nor did his flesh see corruption."

13. The resurrection of our bodies from the dead begins in our minds. We must change our ideas about the body, and hold to the truth of its origin and destiny as conceived of God, in whose mind its real being exists. The spiritual body of man is the conception of Divine Mind, the creation of Spirit for us. Our work is to make this spiritual body manifest.

14. When we have the right understanding of creation, and, with the help of this understanding, begin the redemption of the body, the Spirit of God quickens the inner life of the whole organism, and we know that the promise in Acts 2:17 is being fulfilled in us: "In the last days, saith God, I will pour forth of my Spirit upon all flesh."

15. The problem before man in the present race consciousness is how to get back to the "Father's house," in which is inexhaustible abundance. As it is by an exercise of the free will inherent in us that we separate ourselves from the Father, so it must be through that same faculty that we again make conscious union with Him. We must realize the foolishness of living in that most external realm where only the husks of things are, and upon which we would fain satisfy ourselves, but cannot. Then let us turn our attention within; by traveling for a season in that

direction we find the source and substance of life.

16. This turning within, after one has for a long time been looking without, is no easy matter. The mind that has been trained to the standards of the formed universe is often slow to grasp the formless. But there is a state of consciousness in the soul that has, through ages of experience, learned about this formless world and is at home in it. Our dreams, visions, and spiritual experiences, of which we seldom speak, come from this inner realm. So it is found that we have a household waiting for us on the subjective side of our being, and its welcome is worth all the effort of our seeking it. "We seek a country from which we came forth," Paul said in substance.

17. Individualize yourself in the highest degree by affirming that in Spirit and in Truth you are all that God is. This is true of man in his spiritual nature, and he must claim the supreme inheritance before he can enter into the mighty mental and spiritual forces that are released from the kingdom of God within man. No one enters the kingdom of God, and sits upon the throne and abides there, until he has the courage and fearlessness to proclaim himself joint heir with Jesus. Then he must prove his dominion by his purity of motive, an unselfish devotion to Truth universal, and a steady industry and patience in overcoming the limitation of his own sense consciousness.

18. Man's true identity is as the perfect-man idea

in Divine Mind. This idea has no mind separate from the one universal realm of ideas. Man must establish himself in the one and only Mind. He came forth from it, and his whole existence depends on it; then why should he not consciously make the mental connection that will establish in himself the harmony and order on which all existence depends?

19. Nearly all religious systems aim to bring about this unity between God and man, and many of them are quite successful in their methods. We owe much to the church, to the education and the help that we have received directly and indirectly through the efforts of spiritual-minded people in all ages. The Truth has pressed upon them, and they have demonstrated it up to their highest understanding of it. We are now in a fuller degree of enlightenment concerning the spiritual laws that govern man and the universe, and consequently we can more definitely and scientifically apply the methods for spiritual development that, in religious systems, are usually followed through faith. To your faith you can now add *understanding*.

20. One's getting back into the Garden of Eden, or taking possession of the Promised Land, is a conscious entering into the subjective part of one's own being. In divine order the will acts upon the body center from within; in the average person this action is through reflection from without. In practice we live outside our body instead of within it. This gives us a very slender hold upon it, and it is in conse-

quence weak and likely to slip away from us on very slight pretexts.

21. Man should constantly affirm: *I AM, and I will manifest, the perfection of the Mind within me.* The first part of the statement is abstract Truth; the second part is concrete identification of man with this Truth. We must learn the law of expression from the abstract to the concrete—from the formless to the formed. Every idea makes a structure after its own image and likeness, and all such ideas and structures are grouped and associated according to their offices. *

22. All ideas pertaining to power group themselves about structures impregnated with power. Such ideas are not attracted to ideas of love. Love has its group, and it builds its structures in a place apart. We have observed certain of the manifest centers in our body; we have recognized and named them as the seat of emotions, as the expression of characteristics supposed to exist in the soul. Love is universally recognized as expressing itself through the heart, and intelligence as expressing itself through the head.

23. In the study of Mind and Spirit, these inner centers of consciousness are concentrated on until they respond to the *I will* and become obedient to it. By this method man finds that he can control and direct every body function and perpetuate it.

24. This is the "regeneration" of the New Testament, a process of body refinement to the point of

physical immortality. Jesus called this estate "the regeneration when the Son of man shall sit on the throne of his glory."

"I AM" REALIZATIONS

(To be used in connection with Lesson Three)

1. "I AM THAT I AM."
2. *I am identity demonstrated.*
3. I AM THAT I AM, *and there is no other besides me.*
4. *I am one with Almightiness.*
5. *I am the substance of Being made manifest.*
6. *I am formed in the perfection of the divine-idea man, Christ Jesus.*
7. *My body is not material; it is spiritual and perfect in all its being.*
8. *Centered and established in the one Mind, I am not disturbed by the falsities without me.*
9. *My identity is in God, and my work is to establish His kingdom within me.*
10. *I can do nothing of myself, "but the Father abiding in me does his works."*
11. *I am striving in all my thoughts and ways to make the image and likeness of God manifest in me.*
12. *My "life is hid with Christ in God."*

The Formative Power of Thought

1. That the body is moved by thought is universally accepted, but that thought is also the builder of the body is not so widely admitted. We know that thought moves the various members of the body, because we have constantly before us manifestations of the close sympathy between thought and act. Before I run, I think that I will run, and my legs begin to move swiftly in imagination before I begin the action outwardly. It was found by a system of experiments made at Harvard University that the thought of running causes the blood to rush into the legs. A man was put flat on his back on a balanced beam, which was adjusted so that the least bit of added weight at head or foot registered on the index. When a perfect balance was attained the man was given a problem in mathematics to solve. Immediately the index showed increased weight at the head, indicating that thought had called the blood there. Then he was told to imagine that he was running, and the index showed added weight shifting to the feet.

2. Here is proof that thought not only moves the external members of the body, but that it controls the fluids flowing within the body. If thought so readily moves the blood from place to place, who shall say that it does not move the nerve fluid, or that still more volatile substance, the magnetic force that pervades all organisms? We affirm that thought con-

40

trols nerve forces and magnetic force, and that it not only moves them but also forms and organizes their activities in the body.

3. Medical authorities of the highest repute tell us that certain organs of the body are self-renewing; that it is a puzzle to them how these parts ever wear out. If you had a sewing machine that constantly replaced the little particles worn away by friction, would that machine ever be destroyed? In health, man's body has this power of replacing worn parts and when it is *in harmony* it never wears out. The harmony referred to is self-adjustment to the law of Being, to the law of divine nature, to the law of God. It does not matter what you call this fundamental principle underlying all life—the important thing is to understand it, and to put yourself in harmony with it.

4. We have often been told that we should be healthy if we conformed to the laws of nature, but no one has been able to tell us just what those laws are. Some have said that this conformity consists in eating the right kind of food, or in drinking the right kind of water in the right sort of way, or in breathing pure air and wearing suitable clothes. We have done all these things, and there is yet something lacking. It is quite evident that we have not, by observing these external adjustments, gotten at the underlying principle of nature. Nature works intelligently, and we shall never be able to conform to her laws until we approach her as we would a wise

and loving mother, who, we know, gladly gives us what we want when we use it wisely. Nature is not a blind force working in darkness and ignorance. All her works indicate intelligence—mind in action. This being true, we perceive that we cannot conform to the laws of nature until we recognize the Mind *through* which she works.

5. Those who have not thought about this proposition, those who have not tried to know and understand the *mental* side of life, are like men walking in broad daylight with their eyes closed. The mind has eyes, and we can see (perceive) the inner intelligence when we look with mind. But those who look wholly with the physical eye are really blind—having eyes, they see not. Man's salvation from sin, sickness, pain, and death comes by his understanding and conforming to the orderly Mind back of all existence. "Ye shall know the truth, and the truth shall make you free."

6. Man is an epitome of Being. Psychology finds his soul responding to all the emotions, sensations, and vibrations of the sentient world about him, and spiritual science discerns that his superconsciousness is inspired with all the ideas fundamental in Divine Mind. Man, then, is the key to God and the universe, and he may know all things by studying his own constitution. Supreme in this constitution is mind. Man must base all his researches on mind, because mind is the starting point of every thought and act.

7. Some metaphysicians teach that man makes

himself, others teach that God makes him, and still others hold that the creative process is a co-operation between God and man. The latter is proved true by those who have had the deepest spiritual experiences. Jesus recognized this dual creative process, as is shown in many statements relative to His work and the Father's work. "My Father worketh even until now, and I work." God creates in the ideal, and man carries out in the manifest what God has idealized. Jesus treats of this relation between the Father and the Son in the 5th chapter of John: "The Son can do nothing of himself, but what he seeth the Father doing: for what things soever he doeth, these the Son also doeth in like manner."

8. Thought is the creative power by which man builds a mentality and a body of perfection. Man understandingly uses his creative thought power by mentally perceiving the right relation of ideas, "what he seeth the Father doing," as stated by Jesus. Thus we see the necessity not only for thinking right thoughts, but also for having a right basis for our thinking. We must think according to universal Principle. The successful mathematician bases all his calculations on the rules of mathematical science; so the successful metaphysician bases his creative thinking on the unlimited ideas of the one Mind. Christianity is a science because it is governed by scientific principles of mind action. These principles are really the foundation of all the various sciences, but these sciences are secondary; divine science is primary.

9. The physical scientist deals with the electron, or molecule, or cell, in his analysis of forms. He postulates that atoms exist, but he has never seen one. He assumes that the realm *beyond* the ken of physical perception is not possible of investigation. The metaphysician, however, delves into the realm where atoms, and molecules, and cells are *formed,* and he not only sees how they are made, but he acquires the ability to make them. He finds that they all are dependent on ideas, and that by using right ideas he can make manifest any form or shape that he may desire. For example, what externally is named *substance* has its source in a mental *idea* of form and shape. What is termed *life* has its source in an *idea* of action. What is termed *intelligence* has its source in an *idea* of knowing. All the manifestations that we see about us are produced in the same way; they have their source in some *idea* in mind, and they can be formed and transformed at will by one who understands and uses this mind power.

10. A study of the mind and its innumerable manifestations reveals often a difference between a thing and the mind in which the thing has its original impetus as an idea. Life in Divine Mind is unlimited as an *idea* back of perpetual, omnipresent action, but by man's thought it may be subjected to many limitations. Substance in Divine Mind is an idea of perfection in form, but man's thought usually caricatures it. Intelligence in Divine Mind is all-knowing, but man's thought has said that there is ignorance, so

ignorance has been demonstrated. But we should not assume that all *manifestation* is good because the originating idea came from Divine Mind. All ideas have their foundation in Divine Mind, but man has put the limitation of his negative thought upon them, and sees them "in a mirror, darkly."

11. Applying this reasoning to individual consciousness, we find just how man thinks his body into disease. Instead of basing his thought on what is true in the absolute of Being, he bases it on conditions as they appear in the formed realm about him, and the result is bodily discord in multitudinous shapes. Pervading all nature is a universal thought substance that is more sensitive than the phonographic record. The mechanical record receives and preserves vibrations of sound, but the thought substance does better than this; it transcribes not only all sounds, but even the slightest vibration of thought.

12. The telephone system of a large city is a good illustration of the manner in which thought works on the organism. The nerves are the wires and the nerve fluids are the electricity. The ganglionic aggregations throughout the body are the substations. The presiding intelligence sends its thought from the head; "Central," at the solar plexus, receives the message and makes connection with the part of the body designated. You think of your stomach; instantly the connection is made with that center and the presiding thought stationed there takes your message and carries it into effect. If the message is,

"You are weak," weakness is recorded. If you say,
"You are strong, vigorous, fearless, spiritual intelligence, life, and substance," that message is tran-
scribed and carried into action.

13. Every part of the body is connected with the
great solar-plexus central station, which is very obedient in carrying out instructions received from the
presiding intelligence in the head. There are several
great subcenters and innumerable minor centers in
the organism. These centers of thought are the
formed ideas of mind that have an affinity for one
another, based upon the attractive power of love,
the binding factor of the organism. Physical science
calls this binding energy centripetal force, but all
forces of whatever character are fundamentally spiritual, and they must be reduced to ideas, thoughts,
and words, in order to be understood.

14. All ideas pertaining to life expression have
their center of action in that part of the body called
the generative system; whatever thought we think or
express in words about *life* is immediately sent to
this generative ganglion and registered there. Not
only are these thoughts registered, but man has, by
repeated thinking, built up an ego, or identity, at
that center. The dominant thought of this identity is
life action in its various phases. The life center is
divine, and should be thought about and used in the
purest, highest way. This will lead to the perfect
manifestation of life in the whole body. All thoughts
about the loss of life, or the weakness of life, or

the impurity of life, should be persistently denied out of mind, and we should make the strongest kind of affirmations of what life is in God. In this way we connect the life center with its spiritual source, and it is restored to divine harmony.

15. A majority of the ills that afflict the body have their origin in erroneous thoughts about life and in misuse of the generative life function. In Genesis the life center is compared to a tree—its roots are in the ground and its branches reach up to the heavens. All the pleasant sensations in the organism are produced by the forces emanating from this center. Along the nerves, or branches, the life center sends its currents of life to the very extremities of the body, and even beyond, into the finer ethers of the soul. The life center is spiritual, but its vibrations are so subtle (serpentlike) that man is tempted to eat its fruits, to consume in its pleasant sensations the reserve forces of his organism. His indulgence unfrocks him—takes away his robe of power and mastery and dominion over the physical forces that environ him. Instead of abiding at the center of his body and consciously ruling it and the world of nature without him, he is cast out "from the garden of Eden."

16. By a right understanding, and by using right thoughts and words, man will regain the kingdom within him and will be reinstated in the Garden of Eden. This process of man's taking up power and dominion again is now being carried out in all those

who are seeking the righteousness of the Christ consciousness. In this higher-thought realm, all ideas pertaining to the life of man are in harmonious relation, and when we ask in silent thought for this knowledge, our mind is flooded with its light. We apprehend only according to the receptivity, steadfastness, understanding, and persistent faith of our mind. But we *grow* in faith and understanding, and no matter how slowly we seem to be progressing we should never be discouraged or give up. Everyone is heir to this higher-thought consciousness, and all must eventually attain it. When the beauty of this spiritual realm is spread before us we should express gratitude—give thanks to the great Soul of the universe. When the astronomer Kepler realized the grandeur of the laws that were revealed to him, he exclaimed: "O God, I am thinking Thy thoughts after Thee."

AFFIRMATIONS FOR RIGHT THINKING

(To be used in connection with Lesson Four)

1. *"As he thinketh within himself, so is he."*
2. *My heart is righteous toward God.*
3. *Where my thoughts are gathered together in my Christ name, there I am in the midst of them.*
4. *I will think no evil, for Thou art always with me.*
5. *The thoughts of God are His angels: "He shall give his angels charge concerning thee."*

6. *"The thought of foolishness is sin."*

7. *"The thoughts of the righteous are just."*

8. *"Commit thy works unto Jehovah, and thy purposes shall be established."*

9. *"I know the thoughts that I think toward you, saith Jehovah, thoughts of peace, and not of evil."*

10. *"How precious also are thy thoughts unto me, O God!"*

11. *"Search me, O God, and know my heart: try me, and know my thoughts."*

12. *"Bringing every thought into captivity to the obedience of Christ."*

13. *"Finally, brethen, whatsoever things are true, whatsoever things are honorable, whatsoever things are just, whatsoever things are pure, whatsoever things are lovely, whatsoever things are of good report; if there be any virtue, and if there be any praise, think on these things."*

How to Control Thought

1. Each thought of mind is an identity that has a central ego. By this we mean that every thought has a center around which all its elements revolve and to which it is obedient when no higher power is in evidence. Thoughts are capable of expressing themselves—they think. Man thinks, and he thinks into his thoughts all that he is; hence man's thoughts must be endowed with a secondary power of thought.

2. There is, however, a difference between the original thinking and the secondary thought. One has its animating center in Spirit; the other, in thought. One is Son of God; the other is son of man.

3. The one essential fact to understand is that there can be no manifestation without intelligence as a fundamental factor or constituent part. Every form in the universe, every function, all action, all substance—all these have a thinking part that is receptive to and controllable by man. Material science has observed that every molecule has three things: intelligence, substance, and action. It knows where it wants to go, it has form, and it moves.

4. This intelligent principle in all things is the key to the metaphysician's work. He does not concern himself with the action and reaction of the chemistry of matter, nor does he need to know all the intricate laws of electricity and magnetism in order to get the very highest use of them. They are

susceptible to thought through the knowing factor in their construction, and to this susceptibility he appeals. It is through this all-pervading intelligence that man exercises his highest dominion. The scriptural statement of man's power and dominion over all things is true only when his power and dominion are estimated mentally and spiritually.

5. It is the testimony of all philosophers that everything is in a state of construction or destruction. These two states are all-pervading, and they are apparently essential in building the universe. The metaphysician discerns the cause of these two movements to be the "yes" and the "no" of mind. These dual attributes of mind are in evidence everywhere, but they are not understood by those who observe only form instead of Spirit. The positive and negative poles of the magnet are states of mental affirmation and denial. In acid and alkali, in sour and sweet, chemistry is proclaiming "yes" and "no." Day and night, heat and cold, sunshine and shadow, intelligence and ignorance, good and evil, saint and sinner, all are the reflections of mental affirmations and denials. The constructive or destructive factor in all manifestation is "yes" or "no."

6. It is found that, by the use of these mind forces, man can dissolve things by denying their existence, and that he can build them up by affirming their presence. This is a simple statement, but when it is applied in all the intricate thought forms of the universe it becomes complex. The law of mental

denial and affirmation will prove its truth to all those
who persistently make use of it.

7. The power of the mind to build or destroy is
exemplified most strikingly in the human body.
Whatever we affirm as true of us manifests itself
in due season somewhere in the organism. Whatever we deny is taken away, when the law has had
time to work itself out.

8. The body is made of cells; some in a radiant
state, some crystallized into form. The crystallizing
of these radiant thought forms is the result of affirmations in man's mind that his body is material
instead of spiritual. The affirmative state of mind is
a binding, holding process; it involves all thoughts
and all thought manifestations that come within its
scope. If man affirms his unity with the life, substance, and intelligence of God, he lays hold of these
spiritual qualities; if he affirms the reality of matter
and of the physical body he forms a material picture
that works itself out in flesh.

9. Affirmations do not have to be made in set
terms, such as, "*I affirm my body to be spiritual*";
the general trend of the mind, the sum total of
thought in all its aspects, aggregates the affirmations
that fix and crystallize thoughts into forms. The universal desire and striving of men and women for
material possessions is the strongest kind of affirmation, affecting both mind and body in a marked degree. Stomach troubles and constipation seem to be
common complaints with those who are financially

grasping. The tense state of mind that this affirmation sets up extends throughout the body; all the muscles, nerves, and organs become fixed and almost immovable. This was forcibly illustrated in a certain banker, who was so grasping that his right hand closed rigidly, so that he could not open it. Again, a set ambition and intense desire to excel in some chosen field of work will produce like results. A dominating will fixed in any direction is a form of affirmation, and it affects the life action in the body organism according to its intensity. Congestion, stiffness, rigidity, may all be traced to excessive affirmation.

10. The metaphysical remedy for this selfish state of mind is denial. Jesus said that man must "Deny himself . . . and follow me." The "me" here referred to is the higher self, the Christ, and the "himself" is personality. Denial is a putting away of the mental error and an entering into conscious relaxation of both mind and body. The healer does not tell the patient that constipation is caused by grasping, stingy states of mind. Instead, he mentally denies these habits and holds the patient open and receptive to the great unselfish Mind of the universe. People do not realize how they are bound by their selfishness, and it is not wise to tell them openly, until they understand the difference between their real being and the mortal personality.

11. Where the "no" phase of mind is too much in evidence, the whole consciousness is in relaxation. This excessive negation makes the thought indefinite

and vacillating, the body weak and flabby. Prolapsus, dropsy, certain forms of kidney complaints, nearly all relaxations in body and functions, are the result of the "I can't" state of mind. For example, if a businessman who for years had been intent on money-making should meet with a large loss and mourn over it, he would have kidney trouble of some kind. He would believe that he had lost his substance, and a void-thought would begin its dissipation of the voiding cells of his body. One who has been very ambitious for the attainment of some office or position, and who has been defeated in that ambition, will usually let go the positive mental pole and drop to the negative. The result is bodily weakness some-where. We speak of such people as having "lost their grip." This is exactly what they have done—their mental relaxation has loosened their grasp upon the organism, and it is in a condition of dissolution. Physicians have marveled that so many public men have diabetes and heart disease. It is because, through defeat, they have dropped from success to discour-agement. The failure state of mind throws the whole organism into a panic, and its functions are weak-ened in their life action. Instead of the tonic of as-piration and hope, there is the enervation of dis-couragement and despair.

12. These are conditions that come to those who trust in the arm of flesh. When the mind of man is set on high, he never gives up or allows defeat to thwart his righteous ambitions. His thought is not

set on selfish attainment, consequently he does not develop a mental vacuum when he meets with loss. To one in spiritual understanding there is no loss. The going and coming of material and intellectual things are but changes in the panorama of life. Changes are constantly taking place and will continue so long as we live in the consciousness of duality, the "yes" and "no" state of existence, which is mortality.

13. The object of man's existence is to demonstrate the Truth of Being. This demonstration takes place through experience; but there are two ways of working out experience. The first is by knowing the law of every process, and the second is by blindly testing the process without understanding the law.

14. The human race made a choice when a certain stage of discretion was attained. An illustration of this statement is the allegory of the Garden of Eden. Adam represents generic man. In his early stages he was under the law of divine knowing—the Lord God was his guide and instructor; he made no mistakes, but lived consciously in divine understanding.

15. All experience develops personal identity— the consciousness of the powers of Being in the self. This is the bringing forth of free will, which is inherent in all. In the course of his demonstrations of Being, man arrives at the place where he feels his own ability, and he knows that he can exercise it without restraint. "Satan" is the personal mind that

tempts man to try experience without knowledge. In divine illumination man does not consciously enter into that dual condition typified by "the tree of the knowledge of good and evil." Good is all; evil is that which might be if man forsook his guiding light. In the serene mind of God there is no duality, no good-and-bad, no understanding-and-ignorance. The brilliancy of all-knowing Mind dissolves all shadows, all negations.

16. It is man's privilege to abide in the light, to know how to work out the problem of existence as accurately as the mathematician who follows, without deviation, the rules of his science. The Lord admonishes the unfolding Adam not to "eat"—not to incorporate into his consciousness the knowledge of duality, good and evil. But, like the child who refuses to take the advice of one who knows, man falls into indulgence of the sense of pleasure and excess. The reaction of sense indulgence is pain. Through these experiences, man comes into a consciousness of an opposite to the good. The dual mentality naturally sets up positive and negative forces in his mind, and these opposing forces are reflected into his body. The commotion is so great that the soul is forced out of its temple—man is put out of the garden, and in time forgets his former Edenic state.

17. Some metaphysicians argue that eating the fruit of the tree of knowledge was a necessary step in man's evolution; that by experience we learn all truth, and that without experience we should always

remain infants. Herein is the difference between the
practical Christian and other men: the one seeks the
guiding light of Spirit in all his ways, while the other
ignores that light and works out his character as did
Adam, in the sweat of his face. Hard experiences
come into our lives because we do not know the law
of harmonious thinking. If we think that evil exists as a power in the world, that it is working in
our lives and in the lives of those about us, we make
it an active force, and it appears to be all that we
imagine it. The poet truly discerned that "there is
nothing either good or bad, but thinking makes it so."

18. Some metaphysicians claim that it is not wise
to make denials; that affirmation includes all the
mental movement necessary to man's perfect development. This position would be tenable if we had
built up our consciousness according to divine law.
The student who has carried his mathematical problem forward without making an error does not find
it necessary to erase. But if he sees where he has
made a wrong computation, what then? Nothing but
an erasure, followed by a right computation, will
bring the correct answer. We have all fallen short of
divine ideals; we must cross out our errors and in-
sert Truth, until our character is brought up to the
Jesus Christ standard.

19. Repentance is a form of denial. The forgive-
ness of sin is an erasure of mortal thought from
consciousness. The joy that comes to the converted
Christian results from the inflow of divine love,

which occurs after the mind has been cleansed by
denial of sin. This is a real experience, which may be
repeated again and again by one who understands
the law of Holy Spirit baptism, until the whole man
is sanctified and freed from sin. Christians think of
the joyous exaltation that marked their conversion
as a special sign from the Lord in recognition of their
change of heart. They look back upon it as an experience that comes but once in a lifetime. But metaphysicians who have studied the law of mind, who
have practiced denials and affirmations as a science,
find that they can throw themselves into this ecstatic
state at will.

20. The personal self is the ego around which
revolve all thoughts that bind us to error. We cannot
cross all out at once, but little by little we cast out
the specific thoughts that have accumulated and
built up the false state of consciousness termed
Judas. In the life of Jesus, Judas represents the false
ego that error thought has generated. This "son of
perdition" is so interwoven into the consciousness
that to kill him at one fell swoop would destroy the
mental entity, so he must be counted as one of the
twelve, even while we know that he "hath a devil."

21. In the symbology of Jesus' life, Judas is represented as the treasurer; he "had the bag." This
means that this ego has possession of the sex, or life,
center in the organism and is using it for its own
selfish ends. Judas was a "thief." The selfish use of
the life and vitality of the organism for the grati-

fication of sense pleasure robs the higher nature, and the spiritual man is not built up. This is the betrayal of Christ, and it is constantly taking place in those who live to fleshly, selfish ends.

22. A time comes, however, when Judas must be eliminated from consciousness. The agony of mind and the final crucifixion of Jesus represent the crossing out wholly of the false ego, Judas.

"I die daily," said Paul. The "I" that dies daily is personal consciousness, formed of fear, ignorance, disease, the lust for material possessions, pride, anger, and the legion of demons that cluster about the personal ego. The only Savior of this one is Christ, the spiritual ego, the superconsciousness. We cannot, in our own strength, solve the great, self-purifying problem, but by giving ourselves wholly to Christ and constantly denying the demands of the personal self, we grow into the divine image. This is the process by which we "awake, with *beholding* thy form."

CLEANSING AND PURIFYING STATEMENTS

(To be used in connection with Lesson Five)

1. *God is good, and God is all, therefore I refuse to believe in the reality of evil in any of its forms.*

2. *God is life, and God is all; therefore I refuse to believe in the reality of loss of life, or death.*

3. *God is power and strength, and God is all; therefore I refuse to believe in inefficiency and weakness.*

4. *I am in authority. I say to this thought, "Go, and he goeth; and to another, Come, and he cometh." (Read Mt. 8:5-13.)*

5. *God is wisdom, and God is all! therefore I refuse to believe in ignorance.*

6. *God is spiritual substance, and God is all; therefore there is no reality in the limitations of matter.*

7. *God is inexhaustible resource, and God is all; therefore I refuse to believe in the reality of lack or poverty.*

8. *God is love, and God is all; therefore I refuse to believe in hate or revenge.*

9. *"He that is slow to anger is better than the mighty; and he that ruleth his spirit, than he that taketh a city."*

The Word

1. In pure metaphysics there is but one word, the Word of God. This is the original creative Word, or thought, of Being. It is the "God said" of Genesis. It is referred to in the lst chapter of John as the Logos. It cannot be adequately translated into English. In the original it includes wisdom, judgment, power, and, in fact, all the inherent potentialities of Being. This divine Logos was and always is in God; in fact, it is God as creative power. The Divine Mind creates under law; that is, mental law. Man may get a comprehension of the creative process of Being by analyzing the action of his own mind. First is mind, then the idea in mind of what the act shall be, then the act itself. In Divine Mind the idea is referred to as the Word.

2. According to Genesis and all other mystical writings bearing upon creation, Divine Mind expresses its Word, and through the activity of that Word the universe is brought forth. Man is the consummation of the Word, and his spirit has within it the concentration of all that is contained within the Word. Jesus is called the Word of God. "The Word became flesh, and dwelt among us (and we beheld his glory, glory as of the only begotten from the Father)." God being perfect, His idea, thought, Word, must be perfect. The perfect Word of God is spiritual man. It is through spiritual man, or the

61

Word of God, that all things are made, are brought
into manifestation." "And without him was not anything made that hath been made." The Word is the
"only begotten" of God, because there is but one
idea of man in Divine Mind, and that idea is the
perfect pattern of man's character.

3. In the 1st chapter of John it is implied that
there are things made that are not after divine ideals,
consequently not real. The creations of the Word of
God are permanent and incorruptible. As an imitator
of Divine Mind, man has power to form and make
manifest whatsoever he idealizes; but unless his
thought is unified with Divine Mind and guided in
its operations by infinite wisdom, his thought forms
are perishable.

4. Mental processes enter into all creations.
Physical science has discovered that every atom has
substance, force, and intelligence; these are the three
constituent parts of mind. Mind is the one and only
creative power, and all attempts to account for creation from any other standpoint are futile. The creative processes of mind are continuously operative;
creation is going on all the time, but the original
plan, the design in Divine Mind, is finished.

5. Man cannot know how the thought, or Word,
works except through his own consciousness; consequently he must understand, control, and put in
order his own word, for through it he comprehends
the Word of God. Our most important study, then,
is our own consciousness. The old Greeks recognized

this and wrote over the door of one of their temples: "Man, know thyself." The self of man is spiritual, and when it is in direct conscious unity with the Father-Mind it has permanent formative power. Even in his ignorant use of thought, man's mind is forming conditions, even to the changing of the face of nature itself. Every thought that goes forth from the brain sends vibrations into the surrounding atmosphere and moves the realm of things to action. The effect is in proportion to the ability of the thinker to concentrate his mental forces. The average thought vibration produces but temporary results, but under intense mind activity conditions more or less permanent are impressed upon the sensitive plate of the universal ether, and through this activity they are brought into physical manifestation.

6. Every idea originating in Divine Mind is expressed in the mind of man; through the thought of man the Divine Mind idea is brought to the outer plane of consciousness. In the organism of man are centers that respond to the divine ideas, as a musical instrument sympathetically responds to musical vibrations. Then through another movement on what is termed the conscious, or most outer, plane of action, the thought takes expression as the spoken word. There is in the formed conscious man, or body, a point of concentration for this word; and through this point the word is expressed in invisible vibrations. For example, at the root of the tongue is a brain center, and through it the mind controls the

larynx, the tongue, and all the other organs used in forming words. Following the creative law in its operation from the formless to the formed, we can see how an idea fundamental in Divine Mind is grasped by the man ego, how it takes form in his thought, and how it is later expressed through his spoken word. If in each step of this process he conformed to the divine creative law, man's word would make things instantly, as Jesus made the increase of the loaves and fishes. But since he has lost, in a measure, knowledge of the steps in this creative process from the within to the without, there are many breaks and abnormal conditions, with more failures than successes in the products.

7. However, every word has its effect, though unseen and unrecognized. Jesus said that a man would be held accountable for "every idle word," and a close observation of the power of mind in the affairs of the individual proves this to be true. What we think, we usually express in words; and our words bring about in our life and affairs whatever we put into them. A weak thought is followed by words of weakness. Through the law of expression and form, words of weakness change to weakness the character of everything that receives them.

8. The nerves are the wires that transmit the mind's messages to all parts of the body, and these parts, being thought formations, carry out, in their turn, the word that has been spoken into them. Talking about nervousness and weakness will produce

corresponding conditions in the body; on the other hand, sending forth the word of strength and affirming poise will bring about the desired strength and poise. Your talking about a weak stomach will make your stomach weak. Your talking about your bad liver will fix that idea in your liver. The usual conversation among people creates ill health instead of good health, because of wrong words. If the words speak of disease as a reality, disintegrating forces are set in action, and these, in the end, shatter the strongest organism, if not counteracted by constructive forces.

9. As an example of the vibratory power of the spoken word, a vocalist can shatter a wineglass by concentrating upon it certain tones. Every time we speak we cause the atoms of the body to tremble and change their places. Not only do we cause the atoms of our own body to change their position, but we raise or lower the rate of vibration and otherwise affect the bodies of others with whom we come in contact. By telling the little child that he looks sick and tired, the mother produces these conditions in the child's mind and body. If the mother addresses words of health, life, and strength to the child, these will set his bodily functions into activity and they will express the harmony of the dominant thought.

10. Thus every word brings forth after its kind. The "seed" is the creative idea inherent in the word, the nature that it inherits from its parent source—God. The enthusiast in floral culture, who hovers

over and talks in loving tones to his flowers, always
has success with them, while his neighbor, who is
cold and indifferent, fails. The mental emanation and
the creative word are the forces that stimulate the
receptive intelligence of nature, and although the
enthusiast may know nothing of the law of mind,
he is using it in its most effective mode, the creative
word. In like manner the spiritual healer mentally
and audibly speaks to the same all-pervading recep-
tacle, and it responds by building up wasted tissues
and weakened functions.

11. Mind is everywhere and its avenues of expression, like the ether waves of radio, run in every
direction. The wonderful discovery that messages
can be sent around the earth without wires should
forever silence those who have been incredulous
when thought transference through a like ether is
claimed. But there is a means by which ideas may
be transmitted even more rapidly than by mental
vibrations, and that is unity with supreme Mind.
This Mind exists as the absolute, the unlimited. In its
consciousness there is no apartness, no separation,
and whoever puts himself into its consciousness can
accomplish things instantly.

12. When the centurion said to Jesus, "Only say
the word, and my servant shall be healed," the
Master said that He had not found so great faith
in all Israel, and His healing word was: "As thou
hast believed, *so* be it done unto thee." We must
have a certain amount of faith in the substance of

the invisible and in its ability to do our will. When Peter recognized in Jesus that inner principle called Christ, the Son of God, the response was: "Flesh and blood hath not revealed it unto thee, but my Father who is in heaven." The Father must have been present to Peter as He was to Jesus, and the "heaven" in which Jesus said that the Father was must also have been there. The fact is, Being is always present. Mortal ignorance and lack of faith prevent our realization of this truth. The more we believe in the wisdom, power, substance, love, and life of the one Mind, the greater is its activity in us and our affairs. Not only should we have faith in the All-Presence, but we should also develop our understanding to the end that we may know why the All-Presence manifests through us. Physical science is today in advance of religion in its recognition of a universal life substance and intelligence. Religion is looking for this mighty Creator away off in some distant heaven, right in the face of the distinct teaching of Jesus that God is Spirit and that His kingdom is within man.

13. But physical science falls short in that it fails to recognize the unity between omnipresent Intelligence and the knowing principle in man. Science is seeking to know intellectually, or from the plane of forms and shapes, that which is of the mind. Physical science has recognized the presence of the creative forces, but it does not know the power that moves them. Divine metaphysics has discovered the moving

power to be the thought and word of man, and is proving the truth of this principle through results in a multitude of directions.

14. The spoken word carries vibrations through the universal ether, and also moves the intelligence inherent in every form, animate or inanimate. It has been discovered that even rocks and all minerals have life. This is proof of the omnipresence of the one animating substance. Man, being the highest emanation of Divine Mind, has great directive power and is really co-operator with God in forming the universe. We should be speaking words of truth to everything, not only to mankind but to the mineral, vegetable, and animal kingdoms. The fine discernment of the poet reveals that "the very stones cry out" where a tragedy has occurred. The all-penetrating ether receives our thoughts and words, like the wax cylinder of the phonograph, only a thousand times more accurately; it preserves them and echoes them back to us in continuous vibrations. There are no secrets and no concealments. Jesus said that what you think and speak in the inner chamber is proclaimed from the housetops, and now we know why this is true. The very walls of your room, aye, even the substance of the atmosphere in that room, are proclaiming over and over the words that you have spoken there, whether you are present or not. For example, a woman rented a room in a certain city. Several nights in succession, just as she fell asleep, she heard a man talking incoherently about the grain

market. This continued for some time, and she mentioned it to the landlady who informed her that the room had been last occupied by a dealer on the board of trade.

15. The power of the word is given man to use. The better he understands the character of God and his own relation to humanity, the more unselfishly will he exercise this power. Some are using it in selfish ways, but this should not deter others who have a better understanding of the law from using it in righteous ways. "If ye shall ask anything of the Father, he will give it you in my name," is a promise that none should ignore. If we need things and if they are necessary to our happiness, it is not sacrilegious to set into action this higher law in attaining them.

16. The curses of the witch and the blessings of the priest have always been believed in by so-called ignorant and credulous people. In the light of modern revelation, the charge of ignorance should be shifted to the unbelieving. The word of one in authority carries weight and produces far-reaching effects. The fiat of the physician that a certain disease must result disastrously to the patient will, when believed, counteract all the healing forces of nature. A pin scratch has resulted in blood poison, because there was no proper denial that such a result might follow.

17. Man has the power to deny and dissolve all disintegrating, discordant, and disease-forming words. Knowledge of this fact is the greatest dis-

covery of all ages. No other revelation from God to man is to be compared with it. You can make yourself a new creature, and you can build the world about you to your highest ideals. Do not fear, but speak to the law supreme the desires of your heart. If your word is selfish, that which will come to you through its use will be unsatisfactory, but you will profit by the experience and thus learn to speak words of righteousness only. But it is your duty as expresser of the divine law to speak forth the Logos, the very Word of God, and cause the Garden of Eden, the everywhere-present Mind-Substance, to manifest for you and in you in its innate perfection.

THE POWER OF WORDS

(To be used in connection with Lesson Six)

1. *"Death and life are in the power of the tongue."*
2. *"The tongue of the wise is health."*
3. *"He that guardeth his mouth keepeth his life."*
4. *"Whoso keepeth his mouth and his tongue keepeth his soul from troubles."*
5. *"A fool's mouth is his destruction, and his lips are the snare of his soul."*
6. *"Seest thou a man that is hasty in his words? There is more hope of a fool than of him."*

7. *"Pleasant words are as a honeycomb, sweet to the soul, and health to the bones."*

8. *"The lips of the wise shall preserve them."*

9. *"Put away from thee a wayward mouth, and perverse lips put far from thee."*

10. *"Shun profane babblings: for they will proceed further in ungodliness, and their word will eat as doth a gangrene."*

11. *"He that would love life, and see good days, let him refrain his tongue from evil, and his lips that they speak no guile."*

12. *"To him that ordereth his way aright will I show the salvation of God."*

13. *"I will take heed to my ways, that I sin not with my tongue: I will keep my mouth with a bridle, while the wicked is before me."*

14. *"What man is he that desireth life, and loveth many days, that he may see good? Keep thy tongue from evil, and thy lips from speaking guile."*

15. *"Every idle word that men shall speak, they shall give account thereof in the day of judgment."*

Spirituality or Prayer and Praise

1. By the employment of many symbols the Bible describes man in his wholeness—Spirit, soul, and body. The symbols used are men, places, tents, temples, and so forth. The name of every person mentioned in the Bible has a meaning representative of that person's character. The twelve sons of Jacob represent the twelve foundation faculties of man. The name of each of these sons, correctly interpreted, gives the development and office of its particular faculty in triune association; that is, its relation to consciousness in Spirit, in soul, and in body. For example, when the sons of Jacob were born, their mothers revealed the character of the faculty which each represented. This is set forth in the twenty-ninth and thirtieth chapters of Genesis.

2. It is written of the birth of Reuben, "Leah conceived, and bare a son, and she called his name Reuben: for she said, Because Jehovah hath looked upon my affliction." The emphasis is upon the word "looked," and by referring to the concordance we find that the meaning of the word *Reuben* is, "One who sees; vision of the son." It is clear that this refers to the bringing forth of sight.

3. "And she conceived again, and bare a son: and said, Because Jehovah hath heard that I am hated." Here the emphasis is upon the word *heard*, and we find that Simeon means, "That hears or

obeys; that is heard." This is the bringing forth of hearing.

4. "And she conceived again, and bare a son; and said, Now this time will my husband be joined unto me." In this case the emphasis is upon the word *joined*. Levi means "unity," which in body is feeling; in soul, sympathy; and in Spirit, love. So each of the twelve faculties in the complete man functions in this threefold degree.

5. What is here described as the birth of the twelve sons of Jacob is the first, or natural, bringing forth of the faculties. A higher expression of the faculties is symbolized in the Twelve Apostles of Jesus Christ. Simon Peter is hearing and faith united. John is feeling and love joined. When we believe what we hear, there is formed in us the substance of the word, which is Peter, a rock, a sure foundation. "Belief *cometh* of hearing, and hearing by the word of Christ."

6. The Bible is a very wonderful book; as man develops in spiritual understanding it reveals itself to him, and he sees why it has been reverenced and called holy by the people. It is a deep exposition of mental laws, and it is also a treatise on the true physiological estate of the body. It shows that the human organism is mind in action, rather than an aggregation of purely material functions. But above all, the Bible explains the spiritual character of man and the laws governing his relation to God. These are symbolically set forth as states of consciousness,

illustrated by parables and allegories. Paul says, referring to the history of Sarah and Abraham, "Which things contain an allegory." It is written of Jesus, "And without a parable spake he nothing unto them: that it might be fulfilled which was spoken through the prophet, saying, I will open my mouth in parables; I will utter things hidden from the foundation of the world." Jesus was Himself a parable. His life was an allegory of the experiences that man passes through in developing from natural to spiritual consciousness; hence the Bible and the prophets can be understood only by those who arrive at that place in consciousness where the writers were when they gave forth their messages. It requires the same inspiration to read the Scriptures with understanding that it required originally to receive and write them.

7. In the 29th chapter of Genesis we read of Jacob's wife, Leah: "And she conceived again, and bare a son: and she said, This time will I praise Jehovah: therefore she called his name Judah." The Hebrew meaning of the word *Judah* is "praise." In Spirit praise, or prayer, the Judah faculty, accumulates ideas. In sense consciousness this faculty is called acquisitiveness; it accumulates material things and when self is dominant, "hath a devil." This is Judas.

8. Each of the twelve faculties has a center and a definite place of expression in the body. Physiology has designated these faculty locations as brain and nerve centers. Spiritual perception reveals them to

be aggregations of ideas, thoughts, and words. Thoughts make cells, and thoughts of like character are drawn together in the body by the same law that draws people of kindred ideas into assemblies and communities. The intellectual man centers in the head; the affectional man lives in the heart; the sensual man expresses through the abdomen. The activities of these indicated regions are subdivided into a multitude of functions, all of which are necessary to the building up of manifest man as he is idealized in Divine Mind.

9. At the very apex of the brain is a ganglionic center, which we may term the throne of reverence or spirituality. It is here that man holds converse with the knowledge in Divine Mind. This center is the place or "upper room" of spiritual consciousness, and is designated in Scripture as Judah. Its office is to pray and praise. The Judah faculty opens the portal of that mysterious realm called the superconsciousness where thought is impregnated with an uplifting, transcendent quality. Every lofty ideal, all the inspiration that elevates and idealizes in religion, poetry, and art, originates here. It is the kingdom of the true and real in all things.

10. The importance of Judah is indicated by his place in the family of Jacob and Leah. Jacob (supplanter) was betrothed to Rachel (ewe). At the time of the espousal the father of Rachel substituted his elder daughter Leah for the covenanted bride. Leah means "weary." The first son of Leah was

"sight"; weariness saw the light of Spirit. The second son was "hearing"; she was able to receive the word. The third son was "union"; she merged with the limitless. The fourth son was "praise." After the birth of Judah, Leah "left off bearing." Praise is the complement of sight, hearing, and unity. It is the redemption of weariness, and from it issues Messiah, the anointed One, Savior of the world. Instead of a supplication, prayer should be a jubilant thanksgiving. This method of prayer quickens the mind miraculously, and, like a mighty magnet, draws out the spiritual qualities that transform the whole man when they are given expression in mind, body, and affairs.

11. Spirituality is one of the foundation faculties of the mind. It is the consciousness that relates man directly to the Father-Mind. It is quickened and enlarged through prayer and through other forms of religious thought and worship. When we pray we look up from within, not because God is off in the sky, but because this spiritual center in the top of the head becomes active and our attention is naturally drawn to it.

12. Prayer is natural to man, and it should be cultivated in order to round out his character. Prayer is the language of spirituality; when developed, it makes man master in the realm of creative ideas. In order to get results from the use of this faculty, right thinking should be observed here as well as elsewhere. To pray, believing that the prayer may or may not be answered at the will of God, is to miss

the mark. It is a law of mind that every idea is fulfilled as soon as conceived. This law holds true in
the spiritual realm. "All things whatsoever ye pray
and ask for, believe that ye receive them, and ye
shall have them." In the light of our knowledge
of mind action, the law expressed in these words
is clear. Moreover, the faith implied is absolutely
necessary to the unfailing answer to prayer. If we
pray asking for future fulfillment, we form that
kind of thought structure in consciousness, and
our prayers are always waiting for that future
fulfillment which we have idealized. If we pray
thinking that we do not deserve the things for
which we ask, these untrue and indefinite thoughts
carry themselves out, and we grow to look upon
prayer with doubt and suspicion. This is called the
prayer of blind faith, but it is not the kind that Jesus
used, because His prayers were answered.

13. It should not be inferred that the will of
Divine Mind is to be set aside in prayer; we are to
pray that the will of God enter into us and become
a moving factor in our life. "Not my will, but thine,
be done," prayed Jesus. The Father does not take our
will from us; rather, He gives us the utmost freedom
in the exercise of the will faculty, and He also im-
parts an understanding of the law, through the
operation of which we can make any condition that
we desire. "Whatsoever ye shall ask in my name,
that will I do," becomes our assurance.

14. One of the offices of spirituality is to aggre-

gate divine ideas. Through this action man draws
absolutely true ideas from the universal Mind. Thus
prayer is cumulative. It accumulates spiritual substance, life, intelligence; it accumulates everything
necessary to man's highest expression. When we pray
in spiritual understanding, this highest realm of
man's mind contacts universal, impersonal Mind; the
very mind of God is joined to the mind of man. God
answers our prayers in ideas, thoughts, words; these
are translated into the outer realms, in time and condition. It is therefore important that we pray with
understanding of the law, important that we always
give thanks that our prayers have been answered and
fulfilled, regardless of appearances. When Jesus mul-
tiplied the loaves and fishes, He prayed, blessed, and
gave thanks. With understanding and realization of
the relation between the idea and the fulfillment of
the idea, He quickened the slow processes of nature,
and the loaves and fishes were increased quickly. We
may not be able to attain at once such speedy operation of the law, but we shall approximate it, and we
shall accelerate natural processes as we hold our ideas
nearer to the perfection of the realm of divine ideas.

15. Praise is closely related to prayer; it is one of
the avenues through which spirituality expresses itself. Through an inherent law of mind, we increase
whatever we praise. The whole creation responds to
praise, and is glad. Animal trainers pet and reward
their charges with delicacies for acts of obedience;
children glow with joy and gladness when they are

praised. Even vegetation grows best for those who praise it. We can praise our own abilities, and our very brain cells will expand and increase in capacity and intelligence when we speak words of encouragement and appreciation to them.

16. "What is seen hath not been made out of things which appear." There is an invisible thought-stuff on which the mind acts, making things through the operation of a law not yet fully understood by man. Every thought moves upon this invisible substance in increasing or diminishing degree. When we praise the richness and opulence of our God, this thought-stuff is tremendously increased in our mental atmosphere; it reflects into everything that our minds and our hands touch. When common things are impregnated with our consciousness of divine substance, they are transformed according to our ideals. Through persistent application of the Judah faculty, a failing business proposition can be praised into a successful one. Even inanimate things seem to receive the word of praise, responding in orderly obedience when, before, they have seemed unmanageable. A woman used the law on her sewing machine, which she had been affirming to be in bad order. It gave her no trouble afterward. A linotype operator received a certain spiritual treatment given him by a healer at a certain hour, and his linotype, which had been acting badly, immediately fell into harmonious ways. A woman living in a country town had a rag carpet on her parlor floor; she had for

years hoped that this carpet might be replaced by a better one. She heard of the law and began praising the old carpet. Greatly to her surprise, inside of two weeks she was given a new carpet from an unexpected source. These are a few simple illustrations of the possibilities latent in praise. Whether the changes were in the inanimate things, or in the individuals dealing with them, does not matter so long as the desired end was attained.

17. Turn the power of praise upon whatever you wish to increase. Give thanks that it is now fulfilling your ideal. The faithful law, faithfully observed, will reward you. You can praise yourself from weakness to strength, from ignorance to intelligence, from poverty to affluence, from sickness to health. The little lad with a few loaves and fishes furnished the seed that, through the prayer and thanksgiving of Jesus, increased sufficiently to feed five thousand people.

18. If we do not receive answers to our prayers it is because we have not fully complied with the law. "Ye ask, and receive not, because ye ask amiss." This does not mean that we ask of the Lord things that we do not need; it means that we miss the mark in the method of asking, that our relation to Divine Mind is not in harmony with the law; the failure is not in God, but in us. We should therefore never be discouraged, but, like Elijah praying for rain, we should persevere until our prayers are answered.

19. All causes that bring about permanent results originate in Spirit. Spirituality, faith, and love

are God-given faculties, and when we are raised in consciousness to their plane they act naturally under a spiritual law that we may not comprehend. There is a law of prayer, which man will eventually recognize and apply as he now recognizes and applies the laws of mathematics and of music.

20. Jesus said, "Whatsoever ye shall ask in my name, that will I do." We ask in His name when we pray in the Jesus consciousness of universal Spirit. He attained unity with Divine Mind, and realized that His thoughts and words were not from Himself, but from God. When we pray in His name we enter into His unity with the Father, and attain the same consciousness that He attained.

21. God is the always present, indwelling Mind. To realize God we must quiet our outer thoughts and enter into the stillness, peace, and harmony of Spirit. "When thou prayest, enter into thine inner chamber, and having shut thy door [outer consciousness], pray to thy Father who is in secret, and thy Father who seeth in secret shall recompense thee." If we make proper connection with Divine Mind in the kingdom of heaven within us, the Father will surely answer our prayers. No good thing will He withhold from us if we comply with the law of righteous asking. "Be still, and know that I am God."

LIVING WORDS TO QUICKEN SPIRITUALITY

1. *"It is the spirit that giveth life; the flesh profiteth nothing."*

2. *"The letter killeth, but the spirit giveth life."*

3. *"The words that I have spoken unto you are spirit, and are life."*

4. *"Ye must be born from above."*

5. *"I am the light of the world." "Ye are the light of the world."*

6. *"Let your light shine before men; that they may see your good works, and glorify your Father who is in heaven."*

7. *"I am the light"* that *"lighteth every man, coming into the world."*

8. *My understanding is illumined by Spirit. I am the light of my consciousness.*

9. *I acknowledge God at all times as the one source of my understanding.*

10. *"Arise, shine; for thy light is come, and the glory of Jehovah is risen upon thee."*

11. *The glory of the Lord is risen upon me, and I walk in the light of life.*

12. *My body is the temple of the living God, and the glory of the Lord fills the temple.*

13. *Christ within me is my glory. The brightness of His presence casts out all the darkness of error, and my whole body is full of light.*

14. *"He that loveth his brother abideth in the light, and there is no occasion of stumbling in him."*

15. *"Jehovah is my light and my salvation; whom shall I fear? Jehovah is the strength of my life; of whom shall I be afraid?"*

16. *"Then shall Thy light break forth as the morning, and thy health shall spring forth speedily."*

ESTABLISHING THE PERFECT SUBSTANCE

(To be used in connection with Lesson Seven)

1. *"And God created man in his own image, in the image of God created he him; male and female created he them."*

2. *My perfection is now established in Divine Mind.*

3. *"Ye therefore shall be perfect, as your heavenly Father is perfect."*

4. *By seeing perfection in all things, I help to make it manifest. "I must be in my Father's house."*

5. *The corruptible flesh is changed into incorruption when it is seen as perfect and pure in Christ.*

6. *I see in mind that perfect character which I desire to be, and thus plant the seed thought that brings forth the perfect man.*

7. *"But we all, with unveiled face beholding as in a mirror the glory of the Lord, are transformed into the same image from glory to glory, even as from the Lord the Spirit."*

8. *"When Christ, who is our life, shall be manifested, then shall ye also with him be manifested in glory."*

9. *My mind is opened anew to the splendor of God's kingdom, and a flood of rich substance now pours itself into my affairs.*

Faith

1. Now faith is assurance of *things* hoped for, a conviction of things not seen. . . . By faith we understand that the worlds have been framed by the word of God, so that what is seen hath not been made out of things which appear.

2. In the 11th chapter of Hebrews, we find the achievements of faith piled mountain high:

By faith Enoch was translated that he should not see death. . . . By Faith Noah . . . prepared an ark to the saving of his house. . . . By faith Abraham, being tried, offered up Isaac. . . . By faith Moses, when he was born, was hid three months by his parents. . . . By faith the walls of Jericho fell down. . . . And what shall I more say? for the time will fail me if I tell of Gideon, Barak, Samson, Jephthah; of David and Samuel and the prophets: who through faith subdued kingdoms, wrought righteousness, obtained promises, stopped the mouths of lions, quenched the power of fire, escaped the edge of the sword, from weakness were made strong, waxed mighty in war, turned to flight armies of aliens. Women received their dead by a resurrection.

3. The idea that faith is something that has to do only with one's religious experience is incorrect. Faith is a faculty of the mind that finds its most perfect expression in the spiritual nature, but in order to bring out one's whole character it should be developed in all its phases. That it is a power is self-evident. People who have faith in themselves achieve

far more than those who do not believe in their own ability. We call this self-faith innate confidence, but confidence is only a form of faith. Belief is another of the expressions of faith. Jesus apparently made no distinction between faith and belief. He said, "Believe ye that I am able to do this?" and "Whosoever . . . shall not doubt in his heart, but shall believe that what he saith cometh to pass; he shall have it." In an analysis of the constituent parts of man's consciousness, we locate belief in the intellect, working in the thought realm without contact with the more interior substance of Spirit, upon which true faith is founded.

4. In Spirit, faith is related to omnipresent substance or assurance. Jesus used the same illustration when He referred to Peter, a type of faith, as a rock upon which He would found His church. Here is proof that faith is closely allied to the enduring, firm, unyielding forms of earth substance. But free faith has power to do, and power to bring about results in the affairs of those who cultivate it.

5. Like the other faculties, faith has a center through which it expresses outwardly its spiritual powers. Physiologists call this center the pineal gland, and they locate it in the upper brain. By meditation man lights up the inner mind, and he receives more than he can put into words. Only those who have strengthened their interior faculties can appreciate the wonderful undeveloped possibilities in man. The physiologist sees the faculties as brain cells,

the psychologist views them as thought combinations, but the spiritual-minded beholds them as pure ideas, unrelated, free, all-potential.

6. Faith can be extended in consciousness in every direction. It will accomplish wonderful things if quickened and allowed free expression in its native realm. When Jesus said, "If ye have faith as a grain of mustard seed, ye shall say unto this mountain, Remove hence to yonder place; and it shall remove; and nothing shall be impossible unto you," He referred to faith's working in spiritual substance. Such results are possible only to the faith that co-operates with creative law. Where faith is centered in outer things, the results are not worthy of mention. Men have named them luck, accident, chance, and the like. Such charms seem to work for a little while, then suddenly change, so it is evident that they are not under any enduring law.

7. When faith is exercised in the intellectual realm, the results are usually profitable to the man of brains. If he has faith in his art, or his science, or his philosophy, it answers his purpose, for a time at least, but it never gets beyond the traditions and experiences of precedent. Intellectual people do no miracles through faith, because they always limit its scope to what the intellect says is law. It is when faith is exercised deep in spiritual consciousness that it finds its right place, and under divine law, without variation or disappointment, it brings results that are seemingly miraculous.

8. Faith has always played a very large part in the experiences of religious people because they have given it free scope, expecting great things through it from the Lord. But nearly all faith demonstrations have been the result of a sort of blind confidence that God would carry out whatever was asked of Him. Sometimes a petitioner has been disappointed, and a series of disappointments has usually led to doubt and to the conclusion that God has in some way changed His law. The early Christians were taught by Jesus and His disciples to have faith in God, and they did wonderful, so-called miraculous, works. As time went on and their attention was more and more drawn to worldly things, the Christians of a later day became separated from the spiritual forces within them, and their faith lost its energy. Then they began teaching that miracles were no longer necessary; that God had given them to the early Christians because they did not have the Bible or an organized church. They also taught that the miracles had been given to prove that Jesus was the Son of God.

9. Now we have a fuller understanding of the law of God, and know that whatever has been done once can be done again under like conditions. If Jesus and His disciples and the early Christians did marvelous things through the prayer of faith, we can do likewise. All that is required is perseverance in our use of faith until we make connection with the higher realms of consciousness, where, as Jesus said, though our faith be as small as the smallest of

seeds, it will spring forth and demonstrate its power to carry out every desire into which we infuse it. "Nothing shall be impossible unto you," if your faith is in Spirit, and if your work is in harmony with Divine Mind.

10. The Christian religion has been a great factor in the development of faith in the inner realms of man's being. "Blessed *are* they that have not seen, and *yet* have believed." The power to see in Spirit is peculiar to faith. In its outer expression this power is sight; interiorly it is that which perceives the reality of the substance of Spirit. Mental seeing is knowing; when we perceive the truth of a proposition, we say, "I see, I see," meaning that we mentally discern.

11. Faith in the reality of things spiritual develops the faith center in the brain, called the pineal gland. When this mental eye is illuminated with spiritual faith, it sheds a radiance that hovers like a halo around the head and extends in lessening degree throughout the whole body. "When thine eye is single, thy whole body also is full of light." The halo that the early artists painted around the heads of saints was not imaginary, but real. This illuminating power of faith covers the whole constitution of man, making him master of all the forces centering about spiritual consciousness. Faith and prayer go hand in hand.

12. "The faith which thou hast, have thou to thyself before God. Happy is he that judgeth not him-

self in that which he approveth." Have faith in what you do, and after it is done do not condemn yourself. We all are seeking happiness, contentment, and we know by experience that we are happy when we are in tune with our environment. There is a great variety of ideas that cause us inharmony. We think that if we have money and friends we can be happy; but things do not make happiness. It is our mental attitude toward things that fixes our relation to them, and the better we understand the innate substance of the world about us, the more do we appreciate it.

13. Faith is ever active, and it should be made the truth substance of every idea. We should have faith in our own power, capacity, and ability; if we are to have this faith our thoughts must be centered in the great universal Mind. Success lies in God. Whatsoever is not of faith is sin; then whatsoever is of faith is not sin. This is the new standard of righteousness for the man who would "put on Christ." It is his breastplate, his protection, while he is coming up into knowledge of the absolute good. Sin is a missing of the mark, and we miss the mark by not having faith.

14. Faith in the reality, power, and willingness of the mental and spiritual forces is absolutely essential to success in demonstrating the higher law. Jesus was the herald of a set of laws that will revolutionize the civilization of this world and will produce a new and higher type of man. He spoke of a new condition for the uplift of the race; He called it the

"kingdom of heaven," and He said that it must be built upon the foundation typified by Peter (a rock), which is faith. The development of the faith faculty in the mind is as necessary to the worker in spiritual principles as is the development of the mathematical faculty in the worker in mathematics. Neither of these faculties comes at a bound fully formed into consciousness, but both grow by cultivation. "Increase our faith," said the apostles, and Jesus answered: "Have faith in God."

15. Nearly all readers of Scripture recognize Peter as a type of faith. By studying his experiences we may get suggestions on the development of that faculty in ourselves. The fluctuating allegiance of Peter to Jesus illustrates the growth of faith in one who has had no development of that faculty. Faith and doubt contended for supremacy in Peter, and we wonder why Jesus chose as His chief disciple this vacillating, weak, and cowardly fisherman. But we observe that Peter was enthusiastic, bold at times, receptive and patient under reproof. He had never walked on the water, but when Jesus said, "Come," he boldly went out to meet Him. Doubt entered his mind, and he sank; but the helping hand was extended to him and he was made stronger by the experience. This and many other illustrations in the history of Peter show how faith grows in the mind, and we should not be discouraged if our first efforts fall short of the desired end.

16. A very little faith often produces surprising

results. The forces invisible are much closer than we think, and when we turn our attention in their direction the response is usually so pronounced and so swift that we cannot but feel that a miracle has been performed. A more intimate acquaintance with the divine law convinces us that under it all things are possible if we only *believe*, and if we at the same time conform our thoughts to its principle.

17. Peter (faith), James (judgment), and John (love) were the three apostles who were very close to Jesus, and they are more prominent in His history than any of the others. This indicates that these three faculties are developed in advance of the others, also that they are closely associated. Understanding reveals to us that God is a mind-principle whose foundation is *ideas*. When this character of the creative principle dawns upon us, we see how easy it is to commune with God. Through this communion we almost unconsciously strengthen faith, and we find that one faculty helps another to grow. But there must be room in which to grow, and room is made by love. Selfishness is limitation; it binds man in a little prison called personality. The only way to enlarge one's character and give play to all the faculties is through love. Love enlarges the field of consciousness by leveling the thoughts of enmity and opposition. Make friends with all your adversaries quickly, whether they be persons, thoughts, or things.

18. We   are   constantly   making   conditions

through our thoughts. Some people declare that everything is against them. If they miss a car, they say, "It is always that way," and they build up a state of mind in which everything seems contrary to them.

19. In all our experience we should condemn nothing that comes to us and nothing that we do. We know the law; let us keep it, and not set up any adverse conditions by our thoughts of condemnation. Whatever you are doing, be happy in it. If you are getting wrong results, do not believe in an angry God. You are getting the results of your acts, according to your faith. Be wise; pronounce nothing evil, and only good will come. Shall we call everything good? Yes. If the savage knew this law he could lift himself to a higher consciousness by it. We get out of savagery by idealizing the good.

20. Have faith in the innate goodness of all men and all conditions. Do not condemn, no matter how great the provocation. What you *think,* you create in your own consciousness. Enlarge your range of vision, and you may see good in what now seems evil. God is good and God is all, hence there can be no *real* condition but the good. Why should we waste our time fighting evil? If we build our character upon faith, understanding, and love, with the great I AM as the focal center, we shall become pillars in the temple of God.

FAITH AFFIRMATIONS

(To be used in connection with Lesson Eight)

1. *"Now faith is assurance of things hoped for, a conviction of things not seen."*

2. *Holding continuously to the reality of things spiritual establishes them in mind—they become mental substance.*

3. *I believe in the presence and power of the one Mind, and it is to me substantial intelligence.*

4. *"According to your faith be it done unto you."*

5. *My doubts and fears are dissolved and dissipated; in confidence and peace I rest in God's unchangeable law.*

6. *"Great is thy faith: be it done unto thee even as thou wilt."*

7. *With my mind's eye I see more and more the reality of the true ideas ever existing in divine principle.*

8. *"I believe; help thou mine unbelief."*

9. *Jesus said: "Have faith in God."*

10. *I am saved from pain and sorrow through my unswerving faith in the protection and care of God.*

11. *"Lord, increase our faith."*

12. *My faith grows greater day by day, because it is planted in Truth, and through it the mountains of mortal error are moved into the sea of nothingness.*

13. *The understanding of Spirit clarifies my faith.*

14. *"I know him whom I have believed."* I am persuaded that He is able, that He is willing, that He is eager, to give me whatsoever I ask.

15. My faith comprehends the beauty of wholeness.

16. My faith is of God and in God.

17. *"Go thy way; thy faith hath made thee whole."*

Imagination

1. The teachings about the things of Spirit are said to be mystical. We have thought them so because we have not come into consciousness of the many faculties necessary to comprehend Spirit. Victor Hugo said: "There are no occult or hidden truths; everything is luminous with mind." So we find in the study of Truth that what is called mysterious and occult is simply a range of facts that man has not yet explored. When he expands his mind and takes in a larger horizon, he sees the interrelation of a multitude of hitherto unknown laws which, from his former viewpoint, seemed mysterious.

2. Mind manifests through faculties; if mind is to comprehend increasingly, there must be an increase of these avenues. That man has latent possibilities goes without argument; that there is a limit to the ability of the mind is unthinkable. What a man imagines he can do, that he can do. The doing is a question of adopting the right way. To allow the imagination to drift in daydreams never brings anything to pass. Ideas must be worked up into living, breathing, thinking things. Man can compress his vagrant ideas into visibility as the chemist liquefies and makes visible the invisible atmosphere; but to do this he must, like the chemist, have the necessary machinery.

3. Physiology says that, in order to think, man

96

must have brains. However, thinking is not limited to material brain cells but, like everything else in the universe, has a wide range of expression. There are brains within brains, and cells within cells. All through the body are brain centers, whose offices have not yet been determined. Psychology shows that these nerve centers are acted upon by invisible forces; it teaches that man has what is called a subconscious mind, which transcends the conscious mind in knowledge and in ability. Jesus gives us this still higher teaching concerning our mental powers: Man has a mind called the Lord, transcending both the conscious and the subconscious minds. Yet the harmonious working together of these three seemingly separate minds is necessary to the bringing forth of the latent possibilities of the man.

4. In truth there is but one Mind; in it all things exist. Accurately speaking, man does not have three minds, nor does he have even one mind; but he expresses the one Mind in a multitude of ways. To believe in the possession of an individual mind, and that it is necessary to store up knowledge in it, makes living burdensome. This is why very intellectual people are often impractical and unsuccessful; they have accumulated more knowledge than they have wisdom and power to apply. Like the miser who starves surrounded by his gold, they perish for lack of real understanding. Through thinking of their stored-up knowledge as a personal possession, they have insulated it from the original fount of

wisdom and life, and it has consequently become stale and forceless.

5. There is in man that which, when opened, will place him in direct contact with universal knowledge and enable him instantly and continuously to draw forth anything that he may wish to know. God is our fount of wisdom, even as He is our source of supply. The understanding of the Christ Mind reveals that man of himself knows nothing. Jesus, who developed this higher consciousness, claimed that all His knowledge and power came direct from the Father: "I can of myself do nothing." "The Father abiding in me doeth his works."

6. All that man really needs is the quickening and rounding out of the thinking centers in his consciousness; that having been done, Divine Mind will think through him. This supreme Mind holds man at its center, a perfect instrument through which to express its possibilities. The writer of the first chapter of Genesis says that man is formed in the image and after the likeness of God. He is the *I-am-age,* or the identical I AM of God-Mind in expression. God looks into the mirror of the universe and sees Himself as man; He gives Himself to man, and man in his highest is God manifest. "He that hath seen me hath seen the Father." Thus God gives to His image the power to express all that He is. This not only includes man's ability to think, but also the power to shape and form thought. This formative power of thought requires a distinctive fac-

ulty, which is called the "imagination." The mind makes its forms in a way similar to that in which cooks make biscuits. First is the gathering of the materials, then the mixing, then the biscuit cutting, which gives shape to the substance. In thinking, man accumulates a mass of ideas about substance and life, and with his imagination he makes them into forms.

7. Whatever we mirror in our minds becomes a living, active thing, and through it we are connected with the world about us. Through the work of the imaging faculty, every thought makes a form, and multitudes of thoughts make multitudes of forms. These crowd in upon one another around the central *I-am-age,* and appear in what is called the body. Physiology says that all the organs of the body are made up of cells, and that every cell contains the essential elements of its particular organ. The liver is made of a multitude of liver elements, the heart of heart elements, and so forth. The starting point is an idea, and through the mechanism of the mind (often erroneously called the mechanism of the body) man forms his organism. With this key anyone can unlock the door of his temple and in mind visit all its various rooms and set the furniture in order.

8. The imagination has its center of action in the front brain; it uses what phrenology calls the perceptive faculties. It is really the author of these faculties; size, weight, form, color, and the like are its children. When it flashes its light into the cells that

make up the organs, they at once respond to the thought, and out of substance visible and invisible make forms that correspond to the idea held in imagination. If the idea originates in Spirit, the creation is harmonious and according to law. The nerve centers are so sensitive and receptive to thought that they take impressions from without and make in the ether the forms that correspond to the impressions received. This is an inversion of the creative law, which is that all creations shall have their patterns in the mind. When man allows his imagination to run on in a lawless way, he brings about such discord in mind and body that the flood of error thought submerges his understanding and he is drowned in it. "And Jehovah saw that the wickedness of man was great in the earth, and that every imagination of the thoughts of his heart was only evil continually." "And I, behold, I dō bring the flood of waters upon the earth, to destroy all flesh."

9. All things, including the mind, work from center to circumference. A knowledge of this fact puts man on his guard and causes him to direct that his imagination shall not create things in his mind that have been impressed upon him from without. This does not imply that the outer world is all error, or that all appearance is the creation of finite mind; it means that the outer is not a safe pattern from which to make the members of the body. When Moses was instructed by the Lord to furnish the tabernacle, the command was, "See . . . that thou

make all things according to the pattern that was showed thee in the mount." "The mount" is the place of high understanding in mind, which Jesus called the kingdom of God within us. The wise metaphysician resolves into ideas each mental picture, each form and shape seen in visions, dreams, and the like. The idea is the foundation, the real; when understood and molded by the power of the word, it creates or recreates the form at the direction of the individual I AM. By working with this simple law, man may become an adept or master. By handling the cause of things he attains mastery over things, and instead of giving up to his emotions and feelings, he controls them. Instead of letting his imagination run riot, conjuring up all sorts of situations, he holds it steadily to a certain set of ideas that he wants brought forth. "Thou wilt keep *him* in perfect peace, *whose* imagination *is* stayed *on thee*." (Is. 26:3, margin.)

10. As man develops in understanding, his imagination is the first of his latent faculties to quicken. Esau represents the natural man. Jacob represents the intellectual man supplanting Esau; hence Jacob is called the "supplanter." Historically, he seems a trickster, taking advantage of those of less wisdom, but this incident merely shows how the higher principle appropriates the good everywhere. Imagination was the leading faculty in Jacob's mind. He dreamed of a ladder reaching from earth to heaven, the angels of God ascending and descending upon it. This

is prophecy of union between the ideal and its manifestations, between Spirit and body; the union is
made by pure thoughts of the absolute—the angels
of Jacob's dream. Farther along in his development
Jacob awakened all his faculties, represented by his
twelve sons. Joseph was a dreamer and an interpreter
of dreams. He was the favorite son of Jacob, the
I AM, who gave him a coat of many colors. This is
all representative of the imaging faculty, which
Joseph typifies.

11. The history of Joseph is the history of man's
imagination developed under the divine law. His
dreams were messages from God, and God interpreted them for him; his life is one of the most
interesting and fascinating romances in the Bible.
For a time the way of Joseph was thorny, but through
his obedience to Spirit he reached the highest place
in the king's domain. This shows that man begins the
development of the imagination in the darkness of
materiality and in the depths of ignorance, represented by Joseph's being cast into the pit and sold
into Egypt. Through spiritual understanding, the
"dreamer" becomes the most practical son of the
family; by following his dream interpretations, multitudes are saved from starvation. The individual application of this is: Having our attention fixed on
Spirit, we discern the ebb and flow of the forces in
the organism, and we know how to conserve and
husband our resources.

12. Instead of treating the visions of the night as

idle dreams, we should inquire into them, seeking
to know the cause and the meaning of every mental
picture. Every dream has origin in thought, and
every thought makes a mind picture. The study of
dreams and visions is an important one, because it is
through these mental pictures that the Lord com-
municates with man in a certain stage of his unfold-
ment. Solomon was instructed in dreams. "In Gibeon
Jehovah appeared to Solomon in a dream by night;
and God said, Ask what I shall give thee." In Job
33:15, 16, we read, "In a dream, in a vision of the
night, when deep sleep falleth upon men, in slum-
berings upon the bed; then he openeth the ears of
men, and sealeth their instruction." "Then was the
secret revealed unto Daniel in a vision of the night."
Joseph, the husband of Mary, was told in a dream to
take the young child Jesus and go down into Egypt.
Peter was shown his intolerance in a vision, and
Paul was obedient to the "heavenly vision." God
has instructed all the great and wise in every age in
dreams and visions. "Where there is no vision, the
people cast off restraint."

13. Every form and thing, whether in the ether
or on the earth, represents some idea or mental attitude. The idea is first projected into mind substance, and afterward formed in consciousness. The
mind of man sees all things through thought forms
made by the imagination. The lover idealizes the
object of his affection, and is often disappointed on
close acquaintance. We are always creating ideals

that have existence in our minds alone. A true story is told of a sailor who went on a long voyage and left his affianced behind. He thought of her continuously, and often saw her in his dreams. Finally he began to see and talk to her in his waking state, and she told him many remarkable things. She said that it was her soul that visited him; that her body was in her English home, awaiting his return. After some twenty years he arrived at home, expecting a welcome from his loved one. He was dumfounded to learn that she was married, had a family, and had forgotten him. Out of his own mind substance he had created the object of his affection, which had faithfully reflected all his thoughts about her.

14. Through the power of the imagination we impress upon the body the concepts of the mind. Here are stories of actual occurrences: a woman watched her little daughter pass through a heavy iron gate. The gate swung shut and the mother imagined that it had caught and crushed the little one's fingers. But the child had withdrawn her fingers before the gate struck. The mother felt pain in her own hand, and the next day she found a dark streak across her fingers, in the place where she had imagined that the child's had been crushed. In a secret-society initiation, the candidate was told that the word "coward" was to be branded upon his back with a red-hot iron. A piece of ice was used instead, but the promised brand arose in blistered letters.

15. We could cite cases without number to prove

the power of the imagination in forming and transforming the body. Also, one mind can suggest to another and produce any desired condition, if there be mental receptivity. This can be done most effectively through the hypnotic state, but hypnosis is not always necessary. Experiments prove that we are constantly suggesting all sorts of things to one another, and getting results according to the intensity of the imagination. Thus disease is reflected into susceptible minds by people's merely talking about disease as an awful reality.

16. A man can imagine that he has some evil condition in body or affairs, and through the imaging law build it up until it becomes manifest. On the other hand, he can use the same power to make good appear on every side. The marks of old age can be erased from the body by one's mentally seeing the body as youthful. If you want to be healthy, do not imagine so vain a thing as decrepitude. Make your body perfect by seeing perfection in it. Transient patching up with lotions and external applications is foolish; the work must be an inner transformation. "Be ye transformed by the renewing of your mind."

17. The highest and best work of the imagination is the marvelous transformation that it works in character. Imagine that you are one with the Principle of good, and you will become truly good. To imagine oneself perfect fixes the idea of perfection in the invisible mind substance, and the mind forces at once

begin the work of bringing forth perfection.

18. Paul saw this wonderful law at work in character-forming through imitating Christ: "But we all, with unveiled face beholding as in a mirror the glory of the Lord, are transformed into the same image from glory, to glory, even as from the Lord the Spirit."

PERFECTION IN FORM ESTABLISHED

(To be used in connection with Lesson Nine)

1. *I see my countenance in its divine perfection.*

2. *"Thou wilt keep* him *in perfect peace,* whose *imagination* is *stayed* on thee."

3. *I see perfection in all forms and shapes.*

4. *His Son is the brightness of His glory, and the express image of His person.*

5. *I see the light of the Christ consciousness always.*

6. *I am formed anew every day in my mind and my body.*

7. *Be renewed in the spirit of your mind.*

8. *My spirit is quickened in Christ.*

9. *"In a dream, in a vision of the night . . . he openeth the ears of men, and sealeth their instruction."*

10. *I know the reality back of the shadows.*

Will and Understanding

1. "If any man willeth to do his will, he shall know of the teaching." Man manifests that which exists eternally in Being. We talk about the faculties of man's mind as if they belonged to the individual and had origin in him. Man exists in the one invisible Mind. He may assume to have a mind of his own, but his origin and destiny are in God-Mind.

2. Primal causes are complete, finished, absolute. All that man manifests has its origin in a cause that we name Divine Mind, Spirit, God. This being true in logic and intuition, it is not a difficult matter to arrive at the conclusion that the manifestation proves the character of the cause. In dealing with the faculties of man, the relation between them and the one Mind should not be lost sight of. There is but one Mind, and that Mind cannot be separated or divided, because, like the principle of mathematics, it is indivisible. All that we can say of the one Mind is that it is absolute and that all its manifestations are in essence like itself. This brings us to the true estimate of man, and when we speak of spiritual man, or Christ man, or the son of God, we refer to this original expression of Divine Mind.

3. In analyzing these faculties and in establishing their relation in the individual consciousness, we should clearly understand that they are never separated from their Principle, the Divine Mind. In the

text quoted above, Jesus refers to two of the powers
of man and brings out a certain phase of their relation. *Will* and *know* designate the faculties of
mind that we term will and understanding. Through
appropriation, through expansion and growth in
consciousness, will and understanding would seem to
have their source in individual man. But, however
adapted by man, they can never be divorced from
the mind of Being, in which they exist as essential
members of its wholeness.

4. Individual consciousness is like an eddy in the
ocean—all the elements that are found in the ocean
are also found in the eddy, and every eddy may, in
due course, receive and give forth all that is in the
ocean. As the will of God, man represents I AM
identity. This is individual consciousness, freedom
to act without dictation of any kind, selfhood without consciousness of cause, the power to make or
break without limitation, constructive and destructive ability with a universe of workable potentialities.
The will is the man. Without absolute freedom of
will, man would be an automaton. If his will were
restricted in the least degree on any side, he would
not be perfectly free. We know that God is the Great
Unlimited, and man, His "image" and "likeness,"
must be of the same character; consequently man has
the same freedom that God has to act in the fulfillment of desire. God does not dictate man's acts,
although He may instruct and draw him through
love away from error. The idea that God makes man

do certain things cannot be true in a single instance, because, if it were, man would not be a free agent. If God interfered with man's will in some things, it would follow that He could interfere in any and all things. Logic and observation clearly reveal the freedom of man in everything.

5. Creative thought uses the will to build up individual consciousness. The Lord God, or Jehovah, of Genesis, is the original "I WILL BE THAT I WILL BE." In mind, both Jehovah and Jesus mean I AM. I AM is man's self-identity. I AM is the center around which man's system revolves. When the I AM is established in a certain understanding of its Principle, it is divinely guided in its acts, and they are in harmony with divine law. This is the union of will and understanding. In the Scripture these two are designated as Ephraim and Manasseh, sons of Joseph. Their allotments in the Promised Land were joined, indicating that these faculties work in the body from a single brain center. The center is in the forehead.

6. The will should never be retarded in its development, but should be strengthened along all lines. The idea of breaking the will of children is wholly erroneous. The perfect man is produced by rounding out the will and joining it to the understanding. The idea of giving up the will to God's will should not include the thought of weakening it, or causing it to become in any way less; it properly means that the will is being instructed how to act for the best. Do not act until you know how to act.

"Look before you leap." This does not imply that
one should be inactive and indefinite, waiting for
understanding, as do many persons who are afraid to
act because they may possibly do the wrong thing;
it means that understanding will be quickened and
the will strengthened by the confidence that comes
as a result of knowledge.

7. To strengthen the will, and at the same time
to discipline it along right lines, requires an understanding nothing less than divine. But man can balance his will and his understanding; when he does
this he will always do the right thing at the right
time. Nearly every mistake is the result of will's acting without the cooperation of its brother, understanding. When the will is permitted to act on its
own account, man becomes emotional and willful.
These states of consciousness lead to all kinds of
bodily discord. Willfullness makes tenseness, and a
tense mind ties knots in the nerves, muscles, and ten-
dons of the whole organism. The metaphysician, observing these conditions, treats for relaxation of will
and for a general letting go of the whole system. The
universal treatment for this condition given by Jesus
is, "Not my will, but thine, be done." This surrender
causes personal will to "let go," and a unification of
man's will with God's will takes place. When this is
accomplished, all goes well.

8. Willful persons often complain of a feeling
like that produced by a tight band around the head.
This feeling results from the pressure of thought

substance, which the will has laid hold of and is clinging to with centripetal force. In all such cases, and, in fact, in every sense of pressure, treat against personal willfullness and affirm the divine freedom.

9. Every organ of the body is affected by the action of the will, and when this faculty becomes fixed in a certain attitude, it holds the whole body to its central affirmation. The determination to have one's own way, regardless of the rights of others, tends to stop the free action of the heart; the stomach is then sympathetically affected. Persons affected in these ways seldom realize that they have a set determination as to how things shall be done in their lives, and they are sometimes slow in accepting the higher understanding that is necessary to the untangling of mistakes made by the ignorant will. Contrariness is another name for perverted will. An exaggerated idea of self and its needs takes possession of the mind, and the will is used to carry out this shortsighted policy. The result is a belittling of the whole man. Persons who are contentious for their personal rights place themselves in bondage to material conditions and stop spiritual growth.

10. How shall we bring the divine will to bear? By understanding; by appropriating universal wisdom; by affirming: *Not my will, but thine, be done.* God is potential, unformed will; man is manifest God will, or goodwill. When man links his will with the principle of divine force he has superior executive capacity. He swiftly brings forth

faculties that, under the slow action of human personality, would take ages to develop.

11. There is a knowing quality in Divine Mind.
God is supreme knowing. That in man which comprehends is understanding; it knows and compares
in wisdom. Its comparisons are not made in the
realm of form, but in the realm of ideas. It knows
how to accomplish things. We may know without
experience. The human family has learned by hard
knocks that experience is a severe schoolmaster. In
the allegory of Adam and Eve, we see a picture of
man's falling under the sway of sensation (serpent)
and having to learn by experience. One of the esoteric
meanings of *serpent* is "experience." All the bitter
lessons that come through blundering ignorance can
be evaded when men declare their divine understanding and in it follow the divine guidance.

12. For all willfullness, the healing treatment
should be affirmations of spiritual understanding.
The will is not to be broken, but disciplined. The
absolute freedom of the individual must be main-
tained at all hazards. God is the one principle; we
are all as free to use God as we are free to use the
principles of mathematics or of music. The principle
never interferes, but if it is to be rightly applied we
must develop understanding. Freedom leads to many
errors, but, since it is a part of Being, man must learn
to use it properly; he must learn that the freedom
of the law means control and conservation, not lust
and license.

13. We should be careful not to enter into any healing system that interferes with freedom. Hypnotism is not real healing. Any system that suppresses the will is radically wrong. It is the work of the true healer to instruct the patient, to show cause and remedy from the viewpoint of spiritual understanding. All other methods are temporary. The old states of mind will come again into action unless the causing thought is uncovered and removed. A man may have a paralyzed arm through selfish desire for money, and though he may find temporary relief in mere mental suggestions of health, or hypnotism, he will never get permanent healing until he understands the divine law governing possessions, and conforms thereto.

14. There are people who claim that they are being spiritually developed through mediumship. This is error. If you believe that you are under the control of another's will, if you give up to another will, your own will is gradually weakened. If you continue to submit to the domination of another, you will finally lose control of your own life. The will must be strengthened by being constantly used in divine understanding. Mesmerism weakens the will. Spiritual understanding quickens and makes alive. God never puts anyone to sleep. "Awake, thou that sleepest . . . and Christ shall shine upon thee."

15. Never say, "I don't know," "I don't understand." Claim your Christ understanding at all times, and declare: *I am not under any spell of human*

ignorance. I am one with infinite understanding.
The accumulation of ignorance gathered through
association with ignorant minds can be dissolved by
using the word. You may *know* by simply holding
the thought that you know. This is not egotism, but
spiritual knowing. When you declare divine understanding, you sometimes meet your old line of
thought and are disappointed. Right then continue
to hold to your declaration for *knowing*. Judge not
by appearances. Do not act until you get the assurance; if you keep close to Spirit by affirmation, the
assurance will come. Will it come by voice? No! You
will *know* through the faculty of intuition. Divine
knowing is direct fusion of mind of God with mind
of man. Sometimes we are taught by symbols, visions, and the like, but this is only one of the ways
that Divine Mind has of expressing itself. When
the mind deals with God ideals it asks for no symbols, visible or invisible, but rests on *pure knowing*.
It was in this consciousness that Jesus said: "Father,
I thank thee that thou heardest me. And I knew that
thou hearest me always."

16. A very practical application of the truth
about the will can be made in the matter of self-
control. Those who try to get control through sup-
pressing the personal will fall short. We should be
free to express all that we are. If you are afraid of
any force within you, your fear leads to suppression.
In the true self-control, the will and the understanding both play a part. The feelings and appetites and

passions must be disciplined. They are not merely to be held in check by the will, but they are to be lifted up and developed through the Christ Mind.

17. The problem of self-control is never settled until all that man is comes into touch with the divine will and understanding. You must understand all your forces before you can establish them in harmony. This overcoming is easy if you go about it in the right way. But if you try to take dominion through will, force, and suppression, you will find it hard and will never accomplish any permanent results. Get your I AM centered in God, and from that place of Truth speak true words. In this way you will gain real spiritual mastery and raise your will consciousness from the human to the divine.

18. The will plays the leading part in all systems of thought concentration. The simple statement, *I will to be well,* gathers the forces of mind and body about the central idea of wholeness, and the will holds the center just so long as the I AM continues its affirmation. No one ever died until he let go his will to live, and thousands live on and on through the force of a determined will.

19. The "devil" that we are to overcome is the adverse will, which seeks to master man in the without. This "adversary" troubles us because we strive to maintain personal freedom instead of submitting to divine guidance. Self-confidence is a virtue when founded on the Truth of Being, but when it arises from the personal consciousness it keeps man from

his dominion. Are you trying just from yourself to be free from the traditions of the outer world, or are you resting in the understanding and assurance that you are a son of God? To know yourself as a son of God is to overcome the "devil"—the personal self. The "devil" makes you believe that you are the son of the flesh. To overcome, say: *I put Satan behind me by the realization that God is my Father. I am centered in Him, and all things are under His dominion. I live in the infinite Power that produces all self-control. I have no necessity for controlling people. Events and people are controlled by divine law. There is an eternal law of justice. I am one with that law and I rest in it.*

20. Among the apostles of Jesus, Matthew represents the will, and Thomas the understanding. Matthew was the taxgatherer who sat at the gate, representing the executive part of the government; so the will is the executive faculty of the mind and carries out the edicts of the I AM. All thoughts that go into or out of man's consciousness pass the gate at which sits the will, and if the will understands its office, the character and the value of every thought are inquired into and a certain tribute is exacted for the benefit of the whole man.

21. Thomas, the understanding, is represented as under discipline; that is, not yet in the light of Spirit. The understanding, in its first steps in Truth, wants its lessons and accompanying demonstrations to be couched in terms like those used in the outer

world. When Jesus showed Himself to Thomas, the latter said that he would not believe unless he could see the prints of the nails and feel the wound in the side of the Lord. This double proof was given him, and Jesus said: "Be not faithless, but believing." Thomas was then spiritually awakened and he made the acknowledgment: "My Lord and my God."

22. The people who are being educated in Truth through the written and the spoken word will finally arrive at that place where the true light from Spirit will dawn upon them, and they will, like Thomas, see with spiritual understanding and have proof of the reality of the Christ Mind.

THE ESTABLISHMENT OF WILL AND UNDERSTANDING

(To be used in connection with Lesson Ten)

1. *My understanding is established in Divine Mind.*

2. *"Ye shall know the truth, and the truth shall make you free."*

3. *The will of God is ever uppermost in my consciousness.*

4. *"Not my will, but thine, be done."*

5. *I firmly believe the guiding Intelligence that directs all my thoughts.*

6. *"There is a spirit in man, and the breath of the Almighty giveth them understanding."*

7. *The willfullness and stubborness of the flesh have no power in me. I am obedient to Spirit and receptive to all its secret thoughts.*

8. *"Not . . . of the will of flesh, nor of the will of man, but of God."*

9. *I am willing to change my mind.*

10. *"Be ye transformed by the renewing of your mind."*

11. *The Christ of God is born in my consciousness, and I am glorified in my understanding.*

Judgment and Justice

1. Judge not, that ye be not judged. For with what judgment ye judge, ye shall be judged: and with what measure ye mete, it shall be measured unto you.—*Mt. 7:1,2.*

2. And thou shalt put in the breastplate of judgment the Urim and the Thummim; and they shall be upon Aaron's heart, when he goeth in before Jehovah: and Aaron shall bear the judgment of the children of Israel upon his heart before Jehovah continually—*Ex. 28:30.*

3. The Urim and Thummim (Lights and Perfections). These were the sacred symbols (worn upon the breastplate of the high priest, upon his heart) by which God gave oracular responses for the guidance of His People in temporal matters. What they were is unknown; they are introduced in Exodus without explanation, as if familiar to the Israelites of that day. Modern Egyptology supplies us with a clue; it tells us that Egyptian high priests in every town, who were also its magistrates, wore round their necks a jeweled gem bearing on one side the image of Truth, and on the other sometimes that of Justice, sometimes that of Light. When the accused was acquitted, the judge held out the image of him to kiss. In the final judgment Osiris wears around his neck the jeweled Justice and Truth. The Septuagint translates Urim and Thummim by "Light and Truth." Some scholars suppose that they were the twelve stones of the breastplate; others that they were two additional stones concealed in its fold. Josephus adds to these the two sardonyx buttons, worn on the shoulders, which he says emitted luminous rays when the response was favorable; but the precise mode in which the oracles were given is lost in obscurity.—*Bible Glossary of Antiquities.*

119

4. The law as given by Moses is for the guidance of man in the evolution of his faculties. The figures, personalities, and symbols represent potentialities developed and undeveloped on various planes of consciousness. The high priest stands for spiritual man, officiating between God and sense man. The breastplate in an armor protects the most vital part, the heart. The heart is love, the affectional consciousness in man; it may be subject to the force of weak sympathy, unless balanced by another power in which is discrimination, or judgment.

5. The breastplate had on it twelve precious stones, representing the twelve tribes of Israel. This clearly means that the twelve faculties of the mind must be massed at the great brain center called the solar plexus. It means that all the intelligence of man's faculties must be brought into play in the final judgments of the mind. The Urim and Thummim (Lights and Perfections; under the Egyptian symbology, "Truth and Justice") are the oracular edicts of Divine Mind that are intuitively expressed as a logical sequence of the divine principles, truth and justice.

6. A modern metaphysician would interpret all this as signifying the omnipresence of Divine Mind in its perfect idea, Christ. Truth is ready at all times to give judgment and justice. As God is love, so God is justice. These qualities are in Divine Mind in unity, but are made manifest in man's consciousness too often in diversity. It is through the Christ Mind in

the heart that they are unified. When justice and love meet at the heart center, there are balance, poise, and righteousness. When judgment is divorced from love, and works from the head alone, there goes forth the human cry for justice. In his mere human judgment, man is hard and heartless; he deals out punishment without consideration of motive or cause, and justice goes awry.

7. Good judgment, like all other faculties of the mind, is developed from Principle. In its perfection it is expressed through man's mind, with all its absolute relations uncurtailed. Man has the right concept of judgment, and ideally the judges of our courts have that unbiased and unprejudiced discrimination which ever exists in the Absolute. A prejudiced judge is abhorred, and a judge who allows himself to be moved by his sympathies is not considered safe.

8. The metaphysician finds it necessary to place his judgment in the Absolute in order to demonstrate its supreme power. This is accomplished by one's first declaring that one's judgment is spiritual and not material; that its origin is in God; that all its conclusions are based on Truth and that they are absolutely free from prejudice, false sympathy, or personal ignorance. This gives a working center from which the ego, or I AM, begins to set in order its own thought world. The habit of judging others, even in the most insignificant matters of daily life, must be discontinued. "Judge not, that ye be not judged," said Jesus. The law of judgment works out

in a multitude of directions, and if we do not observe it in small things, we shall find ourselves failing in large.

9. Judging from the plane of the personal leads
into condemnation, and condemnation is always followed by the fixing of a penalty. We see faults in
others, and pass judgment upon them without con-
sidering motives or circumstances. Our judgment is
often biased and prejudiced; yet we do not hesitate
to think of some form of punishment to be meted
out to the guilty one. He may be guilty or not guilty;
decision as to his guilt or innocence rests in the
divine law, and we have no right to pass judgment.
In our ignorance we are creating thought forces that
will react upon us. "With what judgment ye judge,
ye shall be judged." "With what measure ye mete,
it shall be measured unto you." Whatever thought
you send out will come back to you. This is an unchangeable law of thought action. A man may be
just in all his dealings, yet if he condemns others
for their injustice, that thought action will bring him
into unjust conditions; so it is not safe to judge
except in the Absolute. Jesus said that He judged no
man on His own account, but in the Father; that is,
He judged in the Principle. This is the stand which
everyone must take—resting judgment of others in
the Absolute. When this is done the tendency to
condemn will grow less and less, until man, seeing
his fellow man as God sees him, will leave him to
the Absolute in all cases where he seems unjust.

10. The great judgment day of Scripture indicates a time of separation between the true and the false. There is no warrant for the belief that God sends man to everlasting punishment. Modern interpreters of the Scripture say that the "hell of fire" referred to by Jesus means simply a state in which purification is taking place.

11. The word *hell* is not translated with clearness sufficient to represent the various meanings of the word in the original language. There are three words from which "hell" is derived: Sheol, "the unseen state"; Hades, "the unseen world"; and Gehenna, "Valley of Hinnom." These are used in various relations, nearly all of them allegorical. In a sermon Archdeacon Farrar said: "There would be the proper teaching about hell if we calmly and deliberately erased from our English Bibles the three words, 'damnation,' 'hell,' and 'everlasting.' I say—unhesitatingly I say, claiming the fullest right to speak with the authority of knowledge—that not one of those words ought to stand any longer in our English Bible, for, in our present acceptation of them, they are simply mistranslations." This corroborates the metaphysical interpretation of Scripture, and sustains the truth that hell is a figure of speech that represents a corrective state of mind. When error has reached its limit, the retroactive law asserts itself, and judgment, being part of that law, brings the penalty upon the transgressor. This penalty is not punishment, but discipline, and if the transgressor

is truly repentant and obedient, he is forgiven in Truth.

12. Under our civil law, criminals are confined in penitentiaries where it is intended that order, regular habits, and industry be inculcated, and that what seems punishment may prove to be educational. Men are everywhere calling for broader educational methods in our prisons, and this demand is an acknowledgment of the necessity of purification through discipline and training in morals. This purifying process is the penalty taught by Jesus—the judgment passed on sinners—the "hell of fire." When it is received in the right spirit, this fire burns up the dross in character and purifies mind and body.

13. Metaphysicians have discovered that there is a certain relation between the functions and organs of the body and the ideas in the mind. The liver seems to be connected with mental discrimination, and whenever man gets very active along the line of judgment, especially where condemnation enters in, there is disturbance of some kind in that part of the organism. A habit of judging others with severity and fixing in one's mind what the punishment should be causes the liver to become torpid and to cease its natural action; the complexion becomes muddy as a result. "There is therefore now no condemnation to them that are in Christ Jesus . . . who walk not after the flesh, but after the Spirit." This statement held in mind, and carried out in thought and act, will heal liver complaint of that kind. Another form

of thought related to judgment is the vacillating of the mind that never seems to know definitely what is the proper thing to do: "A double-minded man, unstable in all his ways." There must be singleness of mind and loyalty to true ideas. Everyone should have definite ideas of what is just and right, and stand by them. This stimulates the action of the liver, and often gives so-called bad people good health, because they are not under self-condemnation. Condemnation in any of its forms retards freedom of action in the discriminative faculty. When we hold ourselves in guilt and condemnation, the natural energies of the mind are weakened and the whole body becomes inert.

14. The remedy for all that appears unjust is denial of condemnation of others, or of self, and affirmation of the great universal Spirit of justice, through which all unequal and unrighteous conditions are finally adjusted.

15. Observing the conditions that exist in the world, the just man would have them righted according to what he perceives to be the equitable law. Unless such a one has spiritual understanding, he is very likely to bring upon himself physical disabilities in his efforts to reform men. If his feelings come to a point of "righteous indignation," and he "boils" with anger over the evils of the world, he will cook the corpuscles of his blood. Jesus gave this treatment for such a mental condition: "For neither doth the Father judge any man, but he hath given

all judgment unto the Son." This Son is the Christ,
the Universal cosmos; to its equity, man should commit the justice that he wishes to see brought into
human affairs. Put all the burdens of the world
upon the one supreme Judge and hold every man,
and all the conditions in which men are involved,
amenable to the law of God. By so doing, you will set
into action mind forces powerful and far-reaching.

16. If you think that you are unjustly treated by
your friends, your employers, your government, or
those with whom you do business, simply declare
the activity of the almighty Mind, and you will set
into action mental forces that will find expression
in the executors of the law. This is the most lasting
reform to which man can apply himself. It is much
more effective than legislation or any attempt to control unjust men by human ways.

17. Jealousy is a form of mental bias that blinds
the judgment and causes one to act without weighing
the consequences. This state of mind causes the
liver to act violently one day and to be torpid the
next, finally resulting in a "jaundiced eye" and yellow skin. We speak of one "blinded by jealousy," or
"blinded by prejudice." We do not mean by this that
the physical eyes have been put out, but that the understanding has been darkened. Whatever darkens
the understanding interferes in some way with the
purifying processes of the organism, and the fluids
and pigments are congested and the skin becomes
darkened in consequence.

18. The remedy for all this is a dismissal of that poor judgment which causes one to be jealous, and a fuller trust in the great all-adjusting justice of God. In this there should be active trust, which is a form of prayer. The disturbing elements that come into life should be definitely placed in the hands of God. This is much more than mere doubtful trust, or negative expectancy that things will be made right. The Spirit of justice should be appealed to and prayed to with the persistency of an Elijah, or of the Gentile woman whose importunity was rewarded. When the metaphysician sits by his patient with closed eyes he is not asleep, but very much awake to the reality and mental visibility of forces that enter into and make the conditions of the body. This spiritual activity is necessary to the demonstration of the law.

19. Success in the world is largely dependent on good judgment. A prominent businessman was once asked what he considered the most valuable trait of mind in an employee, and he replied: "Good judgment." Everywhere businessmen are looking for people who have judgment equal to the making of quick decisions, on the spur of the moment. Years ago a passenger train was wrecked near a little town in Texas. The station agent in the little town showed his good judgment by settling, right on the spot, with the injured. He did this without authority from headquarters, but he showed such excellent judgment that his ability was recognized and he was

rapidly advanced until he became president of one of
the largest railroad systems in the United States.

20. By clearing your understanding and acknowl-
edging the one supreme Mind in which is all discrimination, you can cultivate the ability of your
mind to arrive quickly at right conclusions. Take the
stand that it is your inheritance from God to judge
wisely and quickly, and do not depart therefrom by
statements of inefficiency in matters of judgment.
When you are in doubt as to the right thing to do
in attaining justice in worldly affairs, ask that the
eternal Spirit of justice shall go forth in your behalf
and bring about and restore to you that which is your
very own. Do not ask for anything but your very
own under the righteous law. Some people unconsciously overreach in their desire for possessions.
When they put the matter into the care of Spirit, and
things do not turn out just as they had expected in
their self-seeking way, they are disappointed and
rebellious. This will not do under the spiritual law,
which requires that man shall be satisfied with justice
and accept the results, whatever they may be. "There
is a divinity that shapes our ends"; it can be co-
operated with by one who believes in things spiritual,
and he will thereby be made prosperous and happy.

JUDGMENT AND JUSTICE STATEMENTS

(To be used in connection with Lesson Eleven)

1. *"Teach me thy way, O Jehovah; and lead me in a plain path."*

2. *The righteousness of the divine law is active in all my affairs, and I am protected.*

3. *"Stand therefore, having girded your loins with truth, and having put on the breastplate of righteousness."*

4. *"The meek will he guide in justice."*

5. *"I will sing of loving kindness and justice."*

6. *My judgment is just, because I seek not my own will, but the will of the Father.*

7. *"Judge not, that ye be not judged."*

8. *"Behold now, I have set my cause in order; I know that I am righeous."*

9. *I believe in the divine law of justice, and I trust it to set right every transaction in my life.*

10. *"There is . . . now no condemnation to them that are in Christ Jesus."*

11. *I no longer condemn, criticize, censure, or find fault with my associates; neither do I belittle or condemn myself.*

Love

1. Behold what manner of love the Father hath bestowed upon us, that we should be called children of God; and *such* we are.

2. He that abideth in love abideth in God, and God abideth in him.

3. He that hath my commandments, and keepeth them, he it is that loveth me: and he that loveth me shall be loved of my Father, and I will love him, and will manifest myself unto him.

4. Love, in Divine Mind, is the idea of universal unity. In expression, love is the power that joins and binds in divine harmony the universe and everything in it.

5. Among the faculties of the mind, love is pivotal. Its center of mentation in the body is the cardiac plexus. The physical representative of love is the heart, the office of which is to equalize the circulation of the blood in the body. As the heart equalizes the life flow in the body, so love harmonizes the thoughts of the mind.

6. We have found that the twelve sons of Jacob represent the twelve faculties of mind. When Levi (love) was brought forth by the human soul (Leah), his mother said: "Now this time will my husband be joined unto me." We connect our soul forces with whatever we center our love upon. If we love the things of sense or materiality, we are joined or attached to them through a fixed law of being. In

the divine order of being, the soul, or thinking part, of man is joined to its spiritual ego. If it allows itself to become joined to the outer or sense consciousness, it makes personal images that are limitations. The Lord commanded Moses to "make all things according to the pattern that was showed thee in the mount." This "mount" is the place of high understanding, or spiritual consciousness, whose center of action is in the very apex of the brain.

7. In the regeneration, our love goes through a transformation, which broadens, strengthens, and deepens it. We no longer confine love to family, friends, and personal relations, but expand it to include all things. The denial of human relationships seems at first glance to be a repudiation of the family group, but it is merely a cleansing of the mind from limited ideas of love when this faculty would satisfy itself solely by means of human kinship. If God is the Father of all, then men and women are brothers and sisters in a universal family, and he who sees spiritually should open his heart and cultivate that inclusive love which God has given as the unifying element in the human family. Just to the extent that we separate ourselves into families, cliques, and religious factions we put away God's love. Unless there is specific denial along every line of human-thought bondage, one will still be under the law of sense. Direct affirmation of spiritual unity, based upon obedience, should be made by everyone who desires to realize this true relation. Jesus said: "Who

is my mother? and who are my brethren? And he
stretched forth his hand towards his disciples, and
said, Behold, my mother and my brethren! For whosoever shall do the will of my Father who is in
heaven, he is my brother, and sister, and mother."

8. Among the apostles of Jesus, John represents love—he laid his head on the Master's bosom.
When this apostle is "called," love is quickened
in consciousness. The calling of this apostle consists in bringing into one's consciousness a right understanding of the true character of love, also in
exercising love in all the relations of life. One should
make it a practice to meditate regularly on the love
idea in universal Mind, with the prayer, *Divine love,
manifest thyself in me.* Then there should be periods
of mental concentration on the love center in the
cardiac plexus, near the heart. It is not necessary to
know the exact location of this aggregation of love
cells. Think about love with the attention drawn
within the breast, and a quickening will follow; all
the ideas that go to make up love will be set into
motion. This produces a positive love current, which,
when sent forth with power, will break up opposing
thoughts of hate, and render them null and void.
The thought of hate will be dissolved, not only in
the mind of the thinker but in the minds of those
with whom he comes in contact in mind or in body.
The love current is not a projection of the will; it
is a setting free of a natural, equalizing, harmonizing
force that in most persons has been dammed up by

human limitations. The ordinary man is not aware that he possesses this mighty power, which will turn away every shaft of hate that is aimed at him. We know that "a soft answer turneth away wrath," but here is a faculty native to man, existent in every soul, which may be used at all times to bring about harmony and unity among those who have been disunited through misunderstandings, contentions, or selfishness.

9. Henry Drummond says that Paul's 13th chapter of I Corinthians is the greatest love poem ever written. In his book based on this chapter, "Love, the Supreme Gift," Professor Drummond analyzes love and portrays its various activities. We quote:

10. THE SPECTRUM OF LOVE. *Love* is a compound thing, Paul tells us. It is like light. As you have seen a man of science take a beam of light and pass it through a crystal prism, as you have seen it come out on the other side of the prism broken up into its component colors—red and blue and yellow and orange, and all the colors of the rainbow—so Paul passes this thing, love, through the magnificent prism of his inspired intellect, and it comes out on the other side broken up into its elements. And in these few words we have what one might call the Spectrum of Love, the analysis of love. Will you observe what its elements are? Will you notice that they have common names; that they are virtues which we hear about every day; that they are things that can be practiced by every man in every place in life; and how, by a multitude of small things and ordinary virtues, the supreme thing, the *Summum bonum*, is made up? The Spectrum of Love has nine ingredients, viz.:

11. Patience—"Love suffereth long." Kindness—"and is kind." Generosity—"Love envieth not." Humility—"Love vaunteth not itself, is not puffed up." Courtesy—"Doth not behave itself unseemly." Unselfishness—"Seeketh not her own." Good Temper—"Is not easily provoked." Guilelessness—"Thinketh no evil." Sincerity—"Rejoiceth not in iniquity, but rejoiceth in the truth."

12. Professor Drummond, in his address on this chapter to Mr. Moody's students gathered at Northfield, Massachusetts, said: "How many of you will join me in reading this chapter once a week for the next three months? A man did that once and it changed his whole life. Will you do it? *Will you?*"

13. Love is more than mere affection, and all our words protesting our love are not of value unless we have this inner current, which is real substance. Though we have the eloquence of men and of angels, and have not this deeper feeling, it profits us nothing. We should deny the mere conventional, surface affection, and should set our mind on the very substance of love.

14. Charity is not love. You may be kindhearted, and give to the poor and needy until you are impoverished, yet not acquire love. You may be a martyr to the cause of Truth and consume your vitality in good works, yet be far from love. Love is a force that runs in the mind and body like molten gold in a furnace. It does not mix with the baser metals—it has no affinity for anything less than itself. Love is patient; it never gets weary or discouraged. Love is

always kind and gentle. It does not envy; jealousy has no place in its world. Love never becomes puffed up with human pride, and does not brag about itself. It is love that makes the refinement of the natural gentleman or lady, although he or she may be ignorant of the world's standards of culture. Love does not seek its own—its own comes to it without being sought.

15. Jesus came proclaiming the spiritual interrelationship of the human family. His teaching was always of gentleness, nonresistance, love. "I say unto you, Love your enemies, and pray for them that persecute you." To do this, one must be established in the consciousness of divine love, and there must be discipline of the mental nature to preserve such a high standard. The divine law is founded in the eternal unity of all things, and "love therefore is the fulfillment of the law." Physical science has discovered that everything can be reduced to a few primal elements, and that if the universe were destroyed it could be built up again from a single cell. So this law of harmony, which has its origin in love, is established in the midst of every individual. "I will put my law in their inward parts, and in their heart will I write it." But before this fixed inward principle can be brought to the surface, man must open the way by having faith in the power of love to accomplish all that Jesus claimed for it.

16. "The love of money is a root of all kinds of evil." The *love* of money, not money itself, is the

root of all kinds of evil. Money is a convenience that saves men many burdens in the exchange of values. Primitive civilization used the cumbersome method of trading products without a money measure of value, while modern progress uses money continually as a medium of exchange. Money is therefore good to the man of sense perception; but when he allows himself to become enamored of it and hoards it, he makes it his god. The erasure of this idea from human consciousness is part of the metaphysician's work. Trusting in God, we have faith in Him as our resource, and He becomes a perpetual spiritual supply and support; but when we put our faith in the power of material riches, we wean our trust from God and establish it in this transitory substance of rust and corruption. This point is not clearly understood by those who are hypnotized by the money idea. When the metaphysician affirms God to be his opulent supply and support and declares that he has money in abundance, the assumption is that he loves money and depends upon it in the same way that the devotees of Mammon do. The difference is that one trusts in the law of God, while the other trusts in the power of Mammon. The man who blindly gives himself up to money *getting* acquires a love for it and finally becomes its slave. The wise metaphysician deals with the money *idea* and masters it.

17. When Jesus said, "I have overcome the world," He meant that by the use of certain words He had dissolved all adverse states of consciousness

in materiality, appetite, and selfishness. Christ is the Word, the Logos. Because the word is·the mind seed from which springs every condition, great stress is laid on the power of the word, both in the Scriptures and in metaphysical interpretations of the Scriptures. The word is the most enduring thing in existence. "Heaven and earth shall pass away, but my words shall not pass away." All metaphysicians recognize that certain words, used persistently, mold and transform conditions in mind, body, and affairs. The word *love* overcomes hate, resistance, opposition, obstinacy, anger, jealousy, and all states of consciousness where there is mental or physical friction. Words make cells, and these cells are adjusted one to the other through associated ideas. When divine love enters into man's thought process, every cell is poised and balanced in space, in right mathematical order as to weight and relative distance. Law and order rule in the molecules of the body with the exactness that characterizes their action in the worlds of a planetary system.

18. Divine love and human love should not be confounded, because one is as broad as the universe and is always governed by undeviating laws, while the other is fickle, selfish, and lawless. It was to this personal aspect of the love center in man that Jesus referred when He said: "Out of the heart of men, evil thoughts proceed." But in the regeneration all this is changed; the heart is cleansed and becomes the standard of right relation among all men. "By

this shall all men know that ye are my disciples, if ye have love one to another." We cannot enter fully into the Christ consciousness so long as we have a grudge against anyone. The mind is so constituted that a single thought of a discordant character tinges the whole consciousness; so we must cast out all evil and resisting thoughts before we can know the love of God in its fullness. "If therefore thou art offering thy gift at the altar, and there rememberest that thy brother hath aught against thee, leave there thy gift before the altar, and go thy way, first be reconciled to thy brother, and then come and offer thy gift."

19. Divine love in the heart establishes one in fearlessness and indomitable courage. "God gave us not a spirit of fearfulness; but of power and love and discipline." A woman who understands this law was waylaid by a tramp. She looked him steadily in the eye and said, "God loves you." He released his hold upon her and slunk away. Another woman saw a man beating a horse that could not pull a load up a hill. She silently said to the man: "The love of God fills your heart and you are tender and kind." He unhitched the horse; the grateful animal walked directly over to the house where the woman was, and put his nose against the window behind which she stood. A young girl sang "Jesus, Lover of My Soul," to a calloused criminal; the man's heart was softened, and he was reformed.

20. The new heaven and the new earth that are now being established among men and nations the

world over are based on love. When men understand each other, love increases. This is true not only
among men, but between man and the animal world,
and even between man and the vegetable world. In
Yellowstone Park, where animals are protected by
our government, grizzly bears come to the house
doors and eat scraps from the table, and wild animals of all kinds are tame and friendly. "The wolf
shall dwell with the lamb, and the leopard shall lie
down with the kid; and the calf and the young lion
and the fatling together; and a little child shall lead
them. . . . They shall not hurt nor destroy in all my
holy mountain; for the earth shall be full of the
knowledge of Jehovah, as the waters cover the sea."

21. Beloved, let us love one another: for love is of
God; and every one that loveth is begotten of God; and
knoweth God. He that loveth not knoweth not God; for
God is love. Herein was the love of God manifested in us,
that God hath sent his only begotten Son into the world
that we might live through him. Herein is love, not that
we loved God, but that he loved us, and sent his Son *to be*
the propitiation for our sins. Beloved, if God so loved us,
we also ought to love one another. No man hath beheld
God at any time: if we love one another, God abideth in
us, and his love is perfected in us: hereby we know that we
abide in him and he in us, because he hath given us of his
Spirit. And we have beheld and bear witness that the Father
hath sent the Son *to be* the Savior of the world. Whosoever
shall confess that Jesus is the Son of God, God abideth in
him, and he in God. And we know and have believed the
love which God hath in us. God is love; and he that abideth
in love abideth in God, and God abideth in him. Herein

is love made perfect with us, that we may have boldness in the day of judgment; because as he is, even so are we in this world. There is no fear in love: but perfect love casteth out fear, because fear hath punishment; and he that feareth is not made perfect in love. We love, because he first loved us. If a man say, I love God, and hateth his brother, he is a liar: for he that loveth not his brother whom he hath seen, cannot love God whom he hath not seen. And this commandment have we from him, that he who loveth God love his brother also.

LOVE DEMONSTRATED

(To be used in connection with Lesson Twelve)

1. *"God is love; and he that abideth in love abideth in God."*
2. *I dwell consciously in the very presence of infinite love.*
3. *God is love, and everyone that loves is born of God.*
4. *I am born of love.*
5. *"Love . . . is the fulfillment of the law."*
6. *I love everybody and everything.*
7. *Faith works by love.*
8. *I have faith in the supreme power of love.*
9. *God has not given us the spirit of fear, but of power, and of love, and of a sound mind.*
10. *I am fearless, powerful, and wise in God's love.*
11. *"Behold what manner of love the Father hath*

bestowed upon us, that we should be called children of God."

12. *I love the Lord my God with all my heart, and with all my mind, and with all my soul, and with all my strength.*

13. *"But now abideth faith, hope, love, these three; and the greatest of these is love."*

STUDY HELPS

and

QUESTIONS

These study helps and questions have been arranged for the convenience of students, whether they are working in class or in the privacy of their own homes. A careful comparison of the students' answers with the text will show how far they have progressed in their study.

LESSON ONE—THE TRUE CHARACTER OF BEING

1. Is there anything scientific about Spirit? Give reasons for your answer.

2. Is it necessary for man's spiritual consciousness to be awake in the beginning of his study of spiritual science? In what attitude should one study?

3. What attitude precedes inspiration of spiritual consciousness? May a certain amount of intellectual study help?

4. What is the starting point in spiritual attainment? What is the Almighty? How does man understand the Almighty?

5. What is one of the most important things that a student of spiritual science can learn? Why?

6. What is the way out of confusion? How does it differ from "blind belief"?

7. How does one get at the very heart of Being?

8. Where is the abode of the Father?

9. Explain God as immanent in the universe. How does this understanding differ from the old idea of God?

10. Does the Power that creates and sustains the universe include man? What is the key to the whole situation?

11. Define Spirit, and explain how it dwells in us.

12. What do we mean by studying "Mind back of nature"?

13. What is man's inheritance, and how can he perpetually draw upon it?

14. What is life in Being?

15. What is the real of the universe? What is practical Christianity?

16. Where should the student start his investigations? Why?

17. What is the point of contact between man and the perfect Mind?

18. What does the parable of the prodigal son typify?

19. Why should the student never be discouraged?

20. Can Truth be imparted? Why?

21. Sum up, in a concise manner, the vital points of this chapter.

LESSON TWO—BEING'S PERFECT IDEA

1. What is spiritual Truth? How does the one Mind create? What is the Logos?

2. What is the law of divine creation?

3. Do the supplications of man change the law of God? Explain.

4. What is the key to our understanding of Divine Mind? Can man come to understand himself or the universe in any other way?

5. Is it important to understand mind and its laws? Why?

6. What is man from the viewpoint of Being?

7. Explain the Trinity and man's place in it.

8. What is the demand of the present age regarding spiritual ideals?

9. What are the three essentials to perfect manhood? What determines the degree to which any one or all of these phases may be expressd?

10. What position does man occupy in relation to God? Is it imperative that man understand this relationship?

11. Is the same faculty required to discern the Christ today that was required in the time of Jesus? If so, what is it?

12. Is it possible for man today to be divinely guided? How is divine guidance brought about?

13. Explain the law of attraction, as applied to mind and ideas.

14. What authority does man require for thinking or speaking beyond prescribed standards?

15. Through what phase of mind do we commune with God?

16. Explain the difference between perceiving and demonstrating one's spiritual sonship. What is the first birth?

17. Explain the first birth; the second birth.

18. What is it to be "born from above"?

19. Explain Jesus' relationship to the Father, and how it was developed.

20. Why does man invent mechanical devices? How will he attain the satisfaction that he seeks in these things?

21. How is the Christ Mind brought into manifestation in the individual?

LESSON THREE—MANIFESTATION

1. What characterizes Christianity as a science?

2. What will bridge the gulf between spiritual and material science?

3. Should the Scriptures be considered allegorical?

4. When read in the light of Spirit, what does the 1st chapter of Genesis portray? What is meant by the words, "and God . . . rested from all his work"?

5. How is the apparent contradiction between the 1st and 2d chapters of Genesis explained?

6. What do the six days of creation mean? How shall we attain the Truth that Jesus said would make us free?

7. How does all creation become harmonious and orderly to man?

8. Describe the difference between the I AM man and the *I will* man. How was man driven out of Eden?

9. What is the physical body, and how is it formed?

10. What will a right idea of the character and origin of the body do for one?

11. Where does the resurrection begin, and what takes place?

12. How shall we get back to the "Father's house"?

13. Where do our dreams, visions, and spiritual experiences come from?

14. How shall we enter into the dominion of the "kingdom" within us?

15. Explain man's true identity?

16. What have the old and the new religious ideas contributed to the solution of our spiritual problems?

17. How shall we get back into the Garden of Eden?

18. Explain the grouping of ideas.

19. How are centers of consciousness brought to respond to the *"I will"?*

20. What is regeneration?

LESSON FOUR—FORMATIVE POWER OF THOUGHT

1. What is the directive power in man?

2. Explain the relation of thought to the functions of the body.

3. Why have we failed to demonstrate perfect health?

4. Upon what must man base his study of God?

5. What is God's work in the creation of man?

6. What part has man in the creation of himself and his world?

7. How does man build his body and his world?

8. Upon what must we base our thinking?

9. Why has the physical scientist failed to demonstrate wholeness and perfection?

10. Explain the difference between life as expressed by man and life in Divine Mind.

11. Upon what do the thoughts act to produce form?

12. Illustrate in your own words how thought works in the organism.

13. Where do ideas pertaining to life have their center of action?

14. How may we connect the life center with its spiritual source, and what is the result of making such connection?

15. What is the cause of imperfect bodies?

16. How may man regain his spiritual dominion?

17. What attitude of mind is conducive to a higher state of consciousness?

LESSON FIVE—HOW TO CONTROL THOUGHT

1. What is the difference between the original thinker and the secondary thought?

2. What is the essential fact in all manifestation?

3. How may man exercise his highest dominion?

4. What are the two fundamental attitudes of mind?

5. What use can man make of these movements of the mind in building his world?

6. What is the result of letting one's thoughts dwell on the acquiring of wealth?

7. Is excessive affirmation advisable? Explain.

8. What is the remedy for the ill effects in the

organism that have come as a result of too much exercise of the affirmative mental attitude?

9. What is the result of excessive denial? What is the remedy for this result?

10. What is the object of man's existence?

11. What is meant by the "Adam" in man?

12. What benefit do we derive from experience?

13. What is "Satan" in man's consciousness?

14. How may man become free from his dual condition?

15. Is experience necessary in man's evolution?

16. What is repentance?

17. What is the meaning of "Deny himself ... and follow me"?

18. Explain the "Judas" in consciousness.

19. Explain the meaning of Paul's words, "I die daily."

20. What is the result of this process of dying daily?

LESSON SIX—THE WORD

1. What is the word?

2. How may man comprehend the creative process?

3. What is the result when the Word is expressed by Divine Mind?

4. Explain how the Word becomes flesh.

5. How may man make his creation perfect?

6. Explain the original plan of creation in Divine Mind.

7. How may man comprehend the word of God?

8. How are divine ideas brought to the outer plane of consciousness?

9. Explain the creative law, from the formless to the formed.

10. What is the result when man's word conforms to the divine law?

11. Explain how we give an account for "every idle word."

12. What determines the character of the word?

13. What ideas make constructive words?

14. Explain the word as the "seed."

15. What is the result of putting oneself into the consciousness of the supreme Mind?

16. What quality must be included in the word, to accomplish results?

17. Wherein does physical science fall short in explaining the plan of creation?

18. Explain the effect of the spoken word.

19. How must we use the word for sure results?

20. Give an illustration of the power of the word.

LESSON SEVEN—SPIRITUALITY, OR PRAYER AND PRAISE

1. What is a symbol?

2. Explain how symbols are used to describe man.

3. What do the twelve sons of Jacob symbolize in man?

4. Explain how a higher expression of the twelve faculties is attained.

5. What is a parable? What is an allegory?

6. How are we able to understand parables and allegories?

7. Is it possible to understand the twelve centers through the intellect?

8. Where is the center of spirituality?

9. What is the work of the Judah faculty?

10. Why should praise be a component part of prayer?

11. Define prayer in your own words.

12. Why do we not receive immediate answer to our prayers?

13. Name some of the benefits to be derived from prayer.

14. What is the effect of praise in prayer?

15. Explain the increasing power of praise.

16. What does it mean to ask "in my name"?

17. Where do we make connection with God, the Father?

18. What is God's will for us?

19. What attitude of mind is most conducive to the effectiveness of prayers?

20. Name five points that you consider essential in prayer.

LESSON EIGHT—FAITH

1. Define faith in your own words.
2. Where does faith find its most perfect expression?
3. Explain the difference between faith and belief.
4. What disciple represents faith? Why?
5. What and where is the center through which faith acts?
6. What is the result of placing faith in outer things?
7. Where must faith be exercised in order to bring the results spoken of by Jesus?
8. What is blind faith? Are the results of blind faith satisfactory?
9. How, in consciousness, is faith increased?
10. What is the inner power of faith? The outer expression?
11. How must faith be used to master the spiritual forces?
12. What fixes our relation to outer things?
13. Where should faith be centered to insure success?
14. Explain, from the experience of Peter on the water, how faith grows.
15. What should be added to faith in order to make it more effective?
16. What two faculties are developed along with faith?
17. Explain how these faculties work with faith.

18. What does it mean to make friends with the "adversary"?

19. Explain how we may have faith in the goodness of all men.

20. Why is faith essential in healing?

LESSON NINE—IMAGINATION

1. How does mind manifest?

2. Explain wherein man is the "image" and "likeness" of God.

3. What power has man as the "image" and "likeness"?

4. Define imagination.

5. Explain how the imaging faculty works on substance.

6. What effect does the imaging power have upon thought?

7. Locate the center of imagination.

8. What faculties of mind does the imagination use, and how?

9. Is it possible to impress these faculties from without, and if so, what is the result?

10. What happens when man allows his imagination to run riot, regardless of law?

11. How do the faculties of the mind work?

12. How can one avoid receiving impressions from without?

13. What is meant by the "mount," as spoken of in the Scriptures?

14. What is the power through which the I AM creates or recreates form?

15. How are we to control the things that we create?

16. What does Jacob represent in consciousness?

17. What does the ladder in Jacob's dream represent?

18. What does Joseph represent, and how did he reach the highest place in the king's domain?

19. What are dreams, and how may they be made useful?

20. What power has the imagination in forming the body? Explain.

21. What is the highest work of the imagination?

LESSON TEN—WILL AND UNDERSTANDING

1. To what does Jesus refer in the text at the beginning of this lesson?

2. Explain how will and understanding work in the individual mind.

3. What does man represent as the will of God?

4. Explain man as a free agent.

5. How do we build individual consciousness?

6. What is the I AM? Explain what the I AM means to you.

7. How may we unify will and understanding?

8. How do we produce the perfect man?

9. What results when the will acts independently of the understanding? Explain.

10. Explain the effect, on the body, of a strong personal will.

11. Explain God and man in relation to will.

12. Define understanding, and show how it works in the mind.

13. What treatment do you suggest for willfullness?

14. Explain why the will should not be broken.

15. Should one try to dominate the will of another, in order to develop him spiritually? Explain.

16. How should you proceed in order to let Divine Mind express itself through you?

17. What is true self-control? How may man exercise it?

18. How may we gain spiritual mastery?

19. What apostle represents will? Explain the use of will in consciousness.

20. Upon what must our understanding be based, that we may be willing to do God's will?

LESSON ELEVEN—JUDGMENT AND JUSTICE

1. Explain the law as given by Moses.

2. Why is judgment necessary in the use of the love faculty?

3. Give the metaphysical meaning of the Urim and Thummim.

4. How may love and justice be balanced in one's life?

5. What is the cause of injustice?

6. Where must judgment be placed, in order to express perfect justice?

7. What is the meaning of "Judge not, that ye be not judged"?

8. Why is man incapable of judging?

9. What is the correct way to judge, as explained by Jesus?

10. What is meant by "the day of judgment"?

11. Explain how and why we are punished.

12. How should we receive punishment?

13. What is the result of the active use of judgment without understanding?

14. What organ of the body is most affected by the active use of judgment, and why?

15. Why should we have definite ideas of justice?

16. What is the result of condemnation?

17. How may we receive perfect justice?

18. Explain the effect of jealousy on the faculty of judgment; give remedy.

19. What is the relation of judgment to success?

20. State the order of procedure in obtaining justice.

———————————

LESSON TWELVE—LOVE

1. Explain love in Divine Mind.
2. What is the work of love in man?
3. What is the result of centering our love on things?
4. How may we realize our true relation to life?
5. Explain the process of love in the regeneration.
6. What apostle represents the faculty of love?
7. Where is the love center?
8. How may thoughts of hatred be overcome in consciousness?
9. What qualities are brought out in man through the activity of the love principle?
10. How shall we make love of real value to ourselves?
11. Explain how love is the fulfilling of the law.
12. What is our relationship to our fellow man when divine love is established in consciousness?
13. When is money really the root of evil?
14. Explain the difference between divine love and human love.
15. How can we know the love of God in its fullness?
16. How shall we proceed to maintain a right relation among all creatures?
17. What is the result when divine love enters into the thought process?
18. Is it possible to approach God while there is aught in the heart against a brother?
19. How may we become established in fearlessness

and courage? Give an illustration from your own experience.

20. What is the unfailing antidote for fear?

———————————

INDEX

Printed U.S.A.   98A-0313-25M-9-88